From Isfahan
to
Wall Street ...and Beyond

My Life's Colorful Journey

by
Ahmad Fakhr

(Some names have been changed to protect the guilty)

First published by Dog Ear Publishing
4010 W. 86th Street, Ste H
Indianapolis, IN 46268
www.dogearpublishing.net

ISBN: 978-145750-615-4

This book is printed on acid-free paper.

Printed in the United States of America

Table of Contents

To my extremely talented and artistic son Darvish,

his equally bright and lovely wife, Leyla

and my precious grandson Pasha Caspian.

I.

1940's

Isfahan, Iran

"The Innocent Years"

I WAS EIGHT YEARS OLD when I dug up my first grave.

It was a warm summer night in 1949, and my uncle Mostafa had come to visit us in the place where I was born, Isfahan, the second largest city in Persia. Uncle Mostafa was a professor at Tehran University, and one of the oldest such institutions in the entire Middle East, and had recently pioneered the zoology department there. Naturally, he was in search of bones.

But I knew none of this when he woke me up well after midnight, holding a finger to his lips and beckoning me outside into the starry night. The fact that I had been dreaming of conquering hordes, or other such things, as small boys are inclined to do, mattered not to Mostafa. I could see a sly fire in his eyes, which meant he was not to be denied.

I always enjoyed Uncle Mostafa's visits.

"Come with me," he whispered. "I have a job for you."

"A mission?" I asked, excited at the thought.

He nodded, smiling, his white teeth glinting in the moonlight. "A *special* mission."

I will never forget following Mostafa through the dusty, quiet streets in the dead of night, the only sounds crickets and the occasional distant voice drifting through the air from the city center. We walked for at least an hour until we reached the outskirts of town, and continued until my uncle finally stopped in a desolate area near the river.

I looked around and was surprised to realize I could not see any evidence of the large city we had only just left behind, save for the ghostly glimmer of distant lights. We might as well have traveled to the other side of the world. It was dark and spooky, but I felt growing excitement as Mostafa lit the paraffin lantern and handed it to me.

"Hold it high, Ahmad."

And then he began to dig.

I hadn't even noticed the small shovel Mostafa had carried under his cloak until he forced its sharpened edge into the stubborn red clay and removed a blade full of moistened earth from the embankment.

I watched, wide-eyed with anticipation, but my uncle did not have to remind me to hold high the lantern. I, too, was on a mission.

When he exposed the first bone, I exhaled sharply, as if I had been holding my breath the entire time. It was the first sound I had made since we left my father's house, and Mostafa turned to me and smiled. "More to come, Ahmad," he said, and continued to work, now slightly more carefully. Eventually he uncovered the bones of entire human skeleton.

"This is what we have come for, Ahmad."

He explained that he needed skeletons for the new zoology department at Tehran University.

I had no idea how he knew exactly where to dig, and it never occurred to me to ask. All I could do was marvel at his find.

We kept digging all night, switching places at times and finally filling up two burlap bags full of bones and skulls, the tales of which would make me the envy of my friends for weeks to come. We walked back home, exhausted, arriving just as the sky began to lighten on the horizon.

After a few hours of sleep, my uncle anxiously but diligently cleaned the bones as I watched enthusiastically. He let me assemble them as he finished, chuckling as I figured out where each piece went. We ended up with two complete human skeletons, which were proudly donated to the zoology department at the University of Tehran, teeth and all. I vowed to become a zoology teacher one day, just like my Uncle Mostafa.

As it turned out, the first grave I opened was also my last, but the memory has remained with me all these years, strange and exciting. And while I never again dug up the bones of a skeleton, human or otherwise, from that moment on I had new respect for the lure of a higher education.

I was the second son born into a middle class family of six. Perhaps arriving second so early in life was what shaped my quiet but competitive disposition. Or maybe having an older brother naturally fuels such ambitions. My father was a supervisor at a large textile factory in Isfahan. The first time he laid eyes on my mother was on their wedding night. She was sixteen at the time and had, before that day, never left her parents' home. It was said she was so frightened that she cried non-stop for two weeks, and told her sisters that living with "this hooligan" for the rest of her life would be an unbearable existence.

An auspicious beginning, to say the least. Thankfully, she gradually learned to put up with him, although not without complaint.

She often mentioned that she should have married a better man, which I suppose was her unconscious nod to feminism, although after he died she did admit that "his presence was preferable to his absence."

In the old days, all marriages in Iran were arranged as such. Typically, the parents of a young man would look for a girl, often younger than their son, who they believed would

My family (I am standing)

make a good match. Then an elder female from the groom's side would simply go to the young woman's house, knock on the door, and ask to speak to the lady of the house. Once inside, she would gradually shift the conversation from the typical pleasantries and hint about seeking their daughter as a bride for a young man in her family. It was a delicate but well practiced ritual, one that allowed both parties to participate without offense.

If the family was receptive, negotiations would commence. This could go on for days and deal with many issues, but of particular interest to both sides were the dowry and other financial matters. Until a consensus was reached, the bride and the groom were kept in the dark about everything. Even when the agreement was finalized, they were informed of the contract but not allowed to see or even speak to each other until the wedding night. After reaching the agreement, the two families would get together for a tea party and happily toast the union outside the presence of the two people on earth most affected by it.

My older brother Reza was born in 1938, I was born in 1940, my sister Shahla in 1943, and the youngest son Ali, in 1949. A fifth child, my younger sister, was born in 1951 but

4

died tragically at the age of three. On a hot summer afternoon in 1954, she drowned in our pool, outside in the yard while the house full of guests were having an afternoon nap.

Many times after that I imagined my sister reaching out to touch her cool reflection on the surface of the water, curious like children of her age, only to watch helplessly as her image faded from view like a polaroid picture in reverse.

No one noticed until my poor mother discovered her life-less body floating in pool, and by then it was too late. That tragic event completely devastated my family, my mother in particular, and she never got over it.

My family lived in a modest house with a maid and a manservant. This was common and traditional in most middle class families in Iran. The maid, Naneh, was an elderly, uneducated woman imported from a nearby village, primarily responsible for cooking and cleaning. She also washed our laundry by hand.

The servant, Abdul Vahab, who had a similar background, was employed to maintain the house, do shopping and carry out any other labor-oriented tasks. I remember him quite vividly from my childhood. He was one of those adults who seem fascinating and exotic to an impressionable child. He was probably in his fifties, which seemed ancient to me, but I suspect he looked much older even to other adults because he was a chain smoker and addicted to opium. He always wore a threadbare but neatly draped jacket, and added an old fedora whenever he went out. Though we lived in the same house, I sometimes wondered if I would recognize him on the street without those worn accouterments.

I remember many nights after supper he would invite me to his tiny room and enthrall me with wild, made-up tales, all the while smoking his opium, which seemed to fuel his stories. I doubt he could read and write, but his vivid imagination more than made up for it.

When we were growing up, he would take Reza and me to the movies once a week. I will never forget the time he took us to see King Kong, in terrifying black and white. I was so frightened I buried my face in his jacket and refused to take it out until the movie was over. In the movie theatres back then, the employees would walk the aisles selling hot boiled potatoes and watermelon seeds. You could hear the constant crackling of the seeds and the floor of the theatre was always littered with their shells.

Most movies were black and white with subtitles, but because a large number of the audience was illiterate, a volunteer would read them out loud so everyone could follow the plot. It really made a difference if the reader was a colorful orator.

———————

Every Friday, the Iranian equivalent to 'the weekend,' my mother would take all her three children to her parent's house for lunch. She would hire a horse-drawn carriage, and after haggling with the driver over the fare for what seemed like hours, she would finally allow us to climb into the buggy. I always enjoyed these rides because it was like a little trip away from home. During one such ride, I fell asleep on my mother's lap and while I was happily dreaming, the horse pulling our carriage farted so loud that I woke up screaming. The sound frightened me so much I cried hysterically all the way to my grandparents' house, and refused to ride on carriages ever again. From that day on, my mother would take us only by bus, or on rare occasions, by taxi. The standard taxi fare was 7 Rials for two passengers, and 15 Rials for four. My mother, however, would argue endlessly with the taxi driver that the fare for four passengers should be only 14 Rials, or 2x7. She would not let us get into the cab until the driver would agree to the 14 Rial fare for the four of us.

My grandparents' kitchen had no electricity, and the only source of light was a round hole in the ceiling through which the sun's rays could enter. They had an old woman from a distant village who did the cooking as well as housekeeping chores. Their cooking fuel was dried bushes and scrubs that peddlers brought from the desert by mule and sold door to door. Burning that stuff caused so much smoke that visibility in the kitchen while the meal was prepared was about the length of the cook's arm, and her eyes were painfully and permanently red, but she was accustomed to it, and had no other options at that time, anyway.

My grandfather, who had a supervisory position in the mayor's office and was responsible for the distribution of narcotics, including opium, was himself an addict and after lunch would smoke both a cigarette and his opium before collapsing for his afternoon nap. Growing and smoking opium was legal in those days, and it was widely used across Iran, especially by the older generation. Ironically, opium had been cultivated in Iran for centuries, but its use only became widespread after foreigners, in particular the British, moved into the country during the nineteenth century and taught by example. Then natural disasters and rising poverty increased its use.

In today's oppressive society, the men of Iran, denied intellectual, economic, and spiritual freedom, have largely reverted to opium use to cope with the boredom, frustration, and pressures of day-to-day life under the current regime. Opium is imported from Afghanistan by the truckload, and the masses despairingly watch their hopes and dreams go up in smoke much as they did a hundred and fifty years ago.

After Abdul Vahab died, one day our new manservant, Morteza, took Reza and me for an outing into the nearby mountains. He loaded both of us on his rickety old bicycle, balancing the two of us on the crossbar as he huffed and puffed halfway up Houh Sofeh outside Isfahan. On the way back, with the three of us rolling faster and faster downhill, he lost control and hit a huge rock, sending everyone flying like ragdolls. The bike broke in half and Reza and I ended up in the hospital with broken bones. With all the opium in his system, he probably felt no pain, but I still carry a scar from that accident on my forehead.

Needless to say, Morteza was replaced. His replacement did not last much longer when he installed a submersible pump in the yard to operate our water well, and had left the wiring exposed without insulating them with electrical tape. Being a curious seven year-old, of course I touched the wires and received a 220 volts jolt, which threw me all the way across the yard. More bruises, a large bump on my forehead to go with my bicycle scar, and another servant lost his job.

I think I preferred the opium smoker.

Due to the stifling heat in the summer, we would sleep outside, protected by a mosquito net. We had never even heard of air conditioning.

On one such night the whole city was stormed by millions of desert locusts, which was quite terrifying. They beat relentlessly against the netting as they swarmed, searching for any and all vegetation. They covered the lights, blanketing the entire city in darkness. All night long we lay awake listening to them; all day long we could barely see three feet in front of us. They swarmed the area for several days, stripping the trees of all their leaves and vanishing just as quickly as they had arrived. I have never seen anything like it, before or since, but such events are not uncommon in desert regions around the world.

As difficult as things were when I was young, we were much better off than my parents growing up. When my mother was about eight years old, she traveled outside her village for the first time, when her father's position was reassigned to the holy city of Mashad. They left in a caravan of camels for the arduous, four hundred mile journey across the formidable desert. Back then, there were no trains or buses or even roads. Everyone traveled by camel, no matter the distance.

Many people were traveling to Mashad for several days of worship and religious activities, and so the caravan was quite large, consisting of over three hundred camels. There was even a 'first class' section of the caravan, which was the lead twenty camels or so, with umbrellas to shelter the riders from the broiling sun.

The 'economy class' camels baked all day in the sun.

Bringing up the rear were the servants, the cook, and the supplies, with tents that were erected each night for the first class members of the caravan. Most of the travelers slept under the open sky.

The entire journey took almost four months each way, and many died along the way, from the heat or disease or even thirst. They traveled for the better part of a year to worship for a single week.

Say what you will of my people, but we are devout.

After hearing that story, it was difficult to complain to my mother about our minor discomforts, although we found ways, I suppose.

Each generation is the same. If things work out as they should, the young grow up to a better life than their parents, but the moaning and complaining never stops.

I know my parents would have never imagined the life I've led, and my children can hardly fathom what things were like for me.

When my brother and I were growing up, our clothing was limited to one pair of pants, two pairs of socks, and one pair of shoes. The trousers were made for us by a tailor using the fabrics that my father brought home from the textile factory where he worked. The pants were typically quite coarse and would scratch the skin badly. The new clothes were given to us once a year at Norouz, the Iranian New Year, which begins at the spring solstice. If anything wore out, it was repaired until the time came for replacement at the next Norouz.

On one occasion when I was eight years-old, my father took me to the Shoe Bazaar, which was a long, dark, dingy corridor lined with shoe makers on either side. Shoes had been cobbled there by hand for centuries.

My father, being the impatient man he was, rushed me through on my first trip to buy black leather shoes, and when we arrived home, I discovered they were mismatched. One pair had a flower stenciled on the toe, while the other one was just plain. I got quite upset by that. Kids everywhere just want to fit in with their peers, and my shoes would definitely be noticed, and not in a good way. But my father absolutely refused to take me back to exchange them, no matter how I begged, and I had to wear them for an entire year. It was quite embarrassing, and I spent the whole time trying to hide my feet in the presence of others.

As we got older, on occasion a group of friends including my brother Reza would go picnicking somewhere either in the mountains nearby or along the Zayiendehroud River, which meandered through town. In the early years we had no transportation, and so we'd leave at daylight and walk for miles, hand carrying all our supplies for the trip. Later on some of us were lucky enough to acquire a used bicycle, and then we'd ride 2 or 3 to a bike, plus supplies.

Picnicking with Friends

These were some of the best experiences of my adolescence. We'd spend the entire day climbing, swimming or fishing in the river. Sometimes we would play cards. For lunch we'd build a fire and barbeque meet on skewers. At dusk we would return home content but totally exhausted. You just don't make friends like you do when you're young.

After my younger brother Ali was born in 1949, my father decided we needed a bigger house. We had one built, with an oval-shaped pool in the middle of the spacious yard. During the summer, my uncle the zoologist and gravedigger would bring his entire family to escape the heat of Tehran and stay with us in Isfahan.

At night, because of the unbearable heat indoors, everyone would either sleep on the flat roof of the house or around the courtyard, outside again with a mosquito net for protection.

At the time, we had a few chickens in the yard that we raised for fresh eggs and occasional cooking. One morning when we woke up, all the chickens were dead. Apparently a fox had somehow snuck into our yard, chased the chickens, caught them one by one, and while we slept, killed them all without waking a single person.

When it rains, it pours.

A year later, my zoologist uncle was a passenger in an open jeep being driven to Isfahan, and was injured badly when he was thrown out onto the gravel road as the vehicle rounded a tight curve. Automobiles had no seat belts in those days. Upon arrival in Isfahan, he was immediately taken to the hospital, covered in blood, and stayed for several days as they attended to his wounds. After being discharged, he was brought to our house where he convalesced for quite some time.

1950 turned out to be a tragic year for my uncle. Shortly after that accident, his wife was hit by a bus and killed on the spot. Apparently, while getting off a public bus in Tehran, the driver pulled away and she fell under the wheels and was run over in the street. The bus driver was apparently racing another driver.

A year later, he married one of his students and had two more children, a boy and girl. His second wife also became a professor, working side by side with her husband at the university. She became an accomplished zoologist in her own right, and she wrote several books, which were used by the students at Tehran University in Iran. She died in St Jose, California at the age of 85.

Not too many years after that, while still relatively young, my uncle contracted tuberculosis and died. I always remembered our little grave-digging expedition with great fondness. I had another uncle, Morteza, who was the oldest of three sons and an officer in the Iranian army during the World War II. In 1944, when I was only four, he and a group of several hundred other officers decided to flee to Russia and seek political asylum. They had been brainwashed and promised the moon by the occupying Russian Troops.

We heard nothing more from him for forty years, until one day my mother received a letter he sent from Beijing. Apparently he had been assigned teaching positions at various communist cities all those years, and had been writing letters that were confiscated, either in Russia or in Iran.

Morteza explained that he had a Russian wife and two sons, and was teaching at Beijing University at that time. He was extremely cultured and intelligent, and spoke several languages fluently, including Russian, Chinese and French, and was also an excellent writer in each language. He had mostly been teaching at Universities in various communist countries. He could not return to Iran during the Shah's reign, because he would have been executed for treason as an army deserter.

Without knowing their sizes, I sent blue jeans for his sons, who were very excited to see real, American Levi's up close for the first time in their lives.

In the mid-eighties after the Iranian Revolution, the window of freedom opened a bit and his letters began to arrive more frequently. After a few years of constantly applying to the Russian Government, he was finally permitted to leave the country. He had been away form his homeland for 45 years.

He first flew to Paris, where my mother rushed to see him. I heard the reunion was all in tears and very emotional.

After some time there, he was finally given clearance from the Iranian Government to return to his home country. Just before he went home, I paid his way to Texas, which was the first time I had seen him since I was a child. I bought him cowboy boots and a ten-gallon hat and took him to my ranch for a few days with my son and other family members visiting. He had a great time, and I was delighted to discover such a smart, well-versed uncle.

He returned to his hometown of Isfahan, where he reunited with his sisters and spent the rest of his life writing and translating books, dying of natural causes at the age of 87. Unfortunately, after he left Russia his sons stopped communicating with him, and his wife died a few years before he passed.

My two favorite uncles led very different lives, but each of them taught me valuable lessons about the importance of perseverance and survival.

Their youngest brother Mojtabah went to Paris on a military scholarship, and completed medical school there before returning to Iran as a doctor, serving a good deal of his career in the army. He was arrested after the revolution, as most army officers were.

What saved him from the firing squad was the fact that years before, during the Shah's regime, a high-ranking Mullah had been tortured and was brought to a military hospital for treatment. A nail had been driven into his skull. It was my uncle Mojtabah who removed the nail and saved his life, and the Mullah returned the favor.

It's rather like Aesop's tale of Androcles and the Lion, which actually originated with Aegypytiacorum, or Wonders of Egypt.

My uncle and the Mullah had each, at different times and by different regimes, been beaten down and stripped of their human rights, and they had each helped the other at a crucial moment. Though man's inhumanity to man seems limitless, it is often a chance meeting or small kindness that resonates across time for the oppressed. Even in the midst of turmoil and strife, there is always hope for a better day.

Behind our new house was a large mulberry tree into which all the neighborhood kids would climb and pick berries when they were in season. One quiet hot sunny afternoon while my father was taking a nap in the shade out in our yard, a young, one-armed neighbor boy climbed the tree to help himself to some white berries. All of a sudden, my father farted so loudly it startled the boy, who fell out of the tree. He was probably a little unsteady up there with only one arm, anyway, but nobody could fart like my father. The "one armed Aboli," as he was called, yelled and cursed, but eventually walked away in pain. Fortunately he did not break any bones.

That boy was fearless. When he played soccer with us, he would use the stump of his amputated arm to push the other players out of his way, and if he got into a fight he'd use the stump like a baton. No one dared get into an argument with him. Many years later, in his 30's, he was found hanging from a noose under a bridge. Obviously he could not have done that himself with only one arm, but they never found out who committed the crime or for what reason. Regardless, he sure made a lot of enemies during his brief time on earth.

Once every twelve months, there was a knock on our door and a mysterious man would deliver something for which we waited the entire year. It was a whole lamb, butchered and ready for roasting. I would rush to the door and hand him the money my mother had given me, and he would disappear once more as quickly as he had appeared. He was known in our neighborhood as 'the smuggler' because he would bypass the required inspections and sell the meat directly to a select few customers more cheaply that at the markets.

If I opened the door when he knocked, I would yell to my mother "the smuggler is here," and she would quickly shush me in fear the neighbors would hear and report us to the authorities.

In those days many services were offered door to door, like sharpening knives, repairing broken china, even bakers who would make cookies and pastries for you in your own kitchen. A few days before the New Year, you could hear shouts from men offering to take the oriental rugs to the river and have them washed.

The streets in my neighborhood were unpaved, and during the winter with snow on the ground, getting around was extremely difficult. I remember one of my friends loved to

Persian rugs getting a spring cleaning in the river

wear suede shoes, which meant walking to school and trying to protect his shoes at the same time was always a dilemma.

I still remember the shouts of enterprising entrepreneurs during the winter months, roaming the streets with spades offering to clear the heavy snow from the flat roofs, which could be damaged from the weight.

II.
1950's

Isfahan, Iran

"Innocense Lost"

WHEN I WAS 12, I became friends with Hamand Biati, the son of a renowned doctor in Isfahan and a good friend of my father. We hit it off immediately and began to spend a lot of time together. Hamand had two older brothers, Narand, who was fond of hunting, and Basand, who was away at medical school, following in his father's footsteps.

I liked playing over at Hamand's house, one of the reasons being that Narand owned a shotgun, and on occasion when he took Hamand off to hunt, I got to tag along. Guns usually fascinate boys, and I was no exception. Another friend of Narand's would often join us with his own shotgun, and so four boys, two guns, and three bicycles would be off before dawn to the mountains outside the city in search of rabbits, pigeons and quail.

Two incidents in particular I remember quite vividly. The first was a cold, dark December morning. It was the kind of pre-dawn cold that made the sun itself want to stay in bed. I was riding on the back of Hamand's bicycle. The wind brushing past my face made my eyes ache, and suddenly I couldn't feel my face. Then I just froze. I was so cold I literally could no longer hold onto the bike, and I collapsed and fell off. I must have passed out, because the next thing I remember, I was lying on warm sand inside a kiln at a brickyard where the bricks were being baked. I was on a mound of sand, but it felt like the softest feather bed in the world. I was so warm and cozy I never wanted to leave. It took me a half hour to dethaw and get my circulation going again, and we resumed out journey and had a successful day of hunting. The others never stopped joking about the time I turned into a popsicle before their very eyes.

The second incident occurred when we were returning from an unsuccessful mountain goat hunt. It was just after dark and we were headed back home in the cold, slightly gloomy that we had not bagged our quarry. To make matters worse, it started to rain very hard, turning the trail into a muddy river of thick, soupy clay. Soon the bikes were clogged with heavy mud, which made riding impossible. But when we hopped off the bikes, we sank down into the mire and couldn't walk, either. The four of us were hopelessly stuck as the freezing rain came down in sheets.

We were still a long way from home, and out of sheer exhaustion more than anything else, I fell asleep right there in the muck. When I opened my eyes a few hours later, a farmer with two mules was loading our disabled bikes and the rest of our gear onto their backs. With heavy clay weighing down our boots, we managed to follow the mules for a couple of miles to the nearest village where the farmer lived, and he provided us with food and shelter for the night.

The rain had stopped by morning, and by the time we woke up, the farmer and his family had washed and cleaned our bikes and set out all our gear, ready for departure. We thanked him and offered what little money we had with us as payment for his kindness, but he would not accept it, and so we happily bicycled to back to Isfahan.

I never saw him again, but the farmer's generosity made a big impression on me, which continues to this day.

Both incidents are comforting reminders of the compassion and generosity of spirit so indicative of my native land.

Hamand and his brothers all had leftish political beliefs, and were semi-active in Tudeh, a quasi-communist party critical of the Shah and his regime. Occasionally they would hold meetings in the suburbs of Isfahan, making speeches and debating solutions to the country's problems. Sometimes I went along on the back of Hamand's bicycle since I did not yet own one.

I will never forget the end result of one of the meetings. It was a big turnout, with a large number of young men who had all bicycled to a private garden to make the usual speeches, most criticizing the government.

The speakers were particularly rousing that day, and afterwards the group decided, in a show of solidarity and power, to ride back to Isfahan all together. As the convoy turned onto the four hundred year-old Khajoo Bridge to cross the Zayiendehroud River, we saw that a barricade had been set up, blocking our way.

And there were two trucks full of police waiting for us.

They jumped out of the vehicles and started swinging their batons, aiming at anyone and everyone they could reach. They beat everyone up and threw the bicycles over the side of the bridge and into the river below. Hamand and I were the youngest and pedaling in the back of the group, so we managed to turn around when we saw what was happening. Hamand pedaled as fast as he could, fueled by terror and pure adrenaline, and I yelled and encouraged him, driven by same, and we managed to get away.

Those who resisted were arrested and taken away. Some were released after a few days, but others, whose names were either already on the "Black List," or put there after the incident, actually served time in jail.

Many in my adopted country of the United States probably can't imagine being arrested simply for belonging to an opposing political party, but it happens quite frequently in other parts of the world.

A BRIEF HISTORY OF IRAN

Once a major empire, Persia, as it had been called, was frequently overrun and its boundaries altered throughout the centuries. It was conquered at one point by the Greeks, Arabs, Mongols, and Turks, among others. Its rich and complicated history dates back to 4000 BC.

In the 6th Century BC, during the Achaemenid Empire, under Cyrus the Great and Darius I, the Persian Empire became the world's first superpower.

For centuries, the Greeks fought with the Persians, until 331 BC when Alexander the Great defeated Darius III, conquered the Persian Empire and torched Persepolis, the King's palace.

During the 7th Century AD, Muslims invaded Persia and the Arab occupation lasted until Genghis Khan and his army of 10,000 Mongols arrived on horseback in 1219, pillaging and burning cities everywhere and killing untold numbers of civilians. Between 1220 and 1258 the population of Iran dropped from 2.5 million to 250,000 as a result of mass extermination and famine.

Then came Tamerlane, who conquered Persia in 1381. He claimed to be a descendant of Genghis Khan, and his campaigns were known for their brutality; many people were slaughtered and cities were destroyed. He died in 1405 during an expedition to China.

The Safavid Empire was Iranians of Azeri and Kurdish origin, and ruled Persia from 1501 TO 1722. The greatest of the Safavid monarchs, Shah Abbas the Great, came to power in 1587 at the tender age of 16. He re-established order within Iran and fought the Ottoman and the Uzbek invaders. He successfully recaptured the northeastern Iran from the Uzbeks, and then turned his attention to the Ottomans defeating them decisively in 1605 and recapturing a good bit of territory in northwestern Iran.

Shah Abbas moved his capital from Qazvin to the more central city of Isfahan in 1598. He beautified the city by building magnificent new Mosques, universities, baths and caravansaries, or roadside inns, along with his Palace Ali Qapu.

Isfahan became one of the most beautiful cities in the world and the center of Safavid architectural achievement. Shah Abbas also imported a few families from Armenia and established a settlement for them in a district named Jolfa on the south side of the Zayienderoud River. Now and again he rode his horse through the settlement to inspect and reassure the Armenian families.

On one such occasion, as he rode back, the river had risen, and as Shah Abbas tried to ride his horse through the rising river, but fell off and almost drowned. Allahverdi Khan, a general and architect rescued him. This prompted the architect to design and build two beautiful bridges that span the same river today, and were widely considered masterpieces of bridge construction. Up until just a few years ago, cars were still allowed to drive over the bridges, but this practice was banned because of the damage it caused the near four hundred year-old structures.

In 1722, an Afshar warlord named Nader Shah deposed the Safavids and crowned himself Shah in 1736. He defeated the Afghans who had invaded Iran in 1719 and expelled the Ottomans. Nader was one of the great conquerors of Asia, and his military acumen enabled his army to take Kandahar and Kabul and march into India in 1739. They killed 30,000 citizens of Delhi and plundered the treasures of the Mughal Emperors, taking 74 elephants loaded with gold, precious stones, and the famous jewel-encrusted Peacock Throne and the giant Koh-I-Noor diamond.

As a gift, he forwarded four of these loaded elephants to Catherine the Great, the empress of Russia, the bulk of which is on display today at the Hermitage Museum in St. Petersburg.

The four elephants that had carried the load to Moscow died during the first winter because the Russians had never seen an elephant, and had no clue how to take care of them.

Nader Shah was assassinated in 1747 by several of his army officers who were commissioned and paid by his nephew, who had been assigned to collect taxes in a southern province but was pocketing some of the money. He was afraid that Nader Shah would kill him if he found out, and so decided to have his uncle killed, instead.

In 1779, the Qajar dynasty triumphed, and Muhammad Khan became the first king of that dynasty. He was the son of a rebellious tribal leader who was killed by Adil Shah, who then castrated the six year-old to prevent him from growing up and aspiring to power. But apparently, that only made him more determined, because he restored Persia to a unity it had not seen since the fall of the Safavid dynasty. He was, however, a man of extreme violence, and killed many of his Muslim subjects. He reduced the town of Tbilisi to ashes and massacred its Christian population, building towers from their skulls.

Never underestimate the temper of an angry eunuch.

Agha Muhammad Khan was assassinated in 1797 in the city of Shusha after 16 years in power. Legend has it that on the night of his death, he ordered his servants to bring him a melon cut into slices. After finishing half, he ordered the other half put away and vowed to his servants that if even one piece was missing in the morning, all three would be beheaded. Later that night, one of the servants forgot and ate a slice of melon. That was either the dumbest servant on earth or the tastiest melon, but in any event, the servants snuck into his chamber and killed Agha Muhammad Khan with a dagger because they believed he would make good on his threat.

In this case, three heads were better than one.

By the 17th century, European countries including Great Britain, Imperial Russia and France had begun establishing colonial footholds in the region, and as a result, Iran lost sovereignty over many of its provinces.

A new era in the History of Persia dawned with the Constitutional Revolution of Iran against the Shah, in the late 19th and early 20th centuries. The Shah managed to remain in power, granting a limited constitution in 1906. The first Majlis (parliament) was convened on October 7, 1906.

The discovery of oil in Khuzestan by the British in 1908 spawned intense interest in Persia by the British Empire, naturally, as well as others, and control of Persia remained contested between the United Kingdom and Russia for some time.

History of Iran

BCE	
Prehistory	
Proto-Elamite period	3200–2800
Elamite dynasty	2800–550
Kassites	16th–12th cent.
Mannaeans	10th–7th cent.
Median Empire	728–550
Achaemenid Empire	550–330
Seleucid Empire	330–150
Parthian Empire	248–CE 226
CE	
Sassanid Empire	226–651
Islamic conquest	637–651
Umayyad Caliphate	661–750
Abbasid Caliphate	750–1258
Tahirid dynasty	821–873
Alavid dynasty	864–928
Sajid dynasty	889/890–929
Saffarid dynasty	861–1003
Samanid dynasty	875–999
Ziyarid dynasty	928–1043
Buyid dynasty	934–1062
Sallarid	942–979
Ma'munids	995–1017
Ghaznavid Empire	963–1187
Ghori dynasty	1149–1212
Seljuq dynasty	1037–1194
Khwarezmid dynasty	1077–1231
Ilkhanate	1256–1353
Muzaffarid dynasty	1314–1393
Chupanid dynasty	1337–1357
Sarbadars	1337–1376
Jalayerid dynasty	1339–1432
Timurid dynasty	1370–1506
Qara Qoyunlu	1407–1468
Aq Qoyunlu	1378–1508
Safavid dynasty	1501–1722/36
Hotaki dynasty	1722–1729
Afsharid dynasty	1736–1750
Zand dynasty	1750–1794
Qajar dynasty	1781–1925
Pahlavi dynasty	1925–1979
Interim Government	1979–1980
Islamic Republic	since 1980

During World War I, the country was occupied by British and Russian forces, but was essentially neutral. In 1919, after the Russian revolution and their withdrawal, Britain attempted to establish a protectorate in Iran, which was unsuccessful.

Finally, the Constitutionalist movement of Gilan and the central power vacuum caused by the instability of the Qajar government resulted in the rise of Reza Shah Pahlavi, who would eventually rule Iran.

In 1921, a military coup established Reza Khan, a Persian officer of the Persian Cossack Brigade, as the dominant figure in the next 20 years. The coup, which was orchestrated by the British, was not actually directed at the Qajar monarchy, but rather targeted at officials in power who controlled the government, namely the cabinet and others with a role in governing Persia. In 1925, after being Prime Minister for a couple of years, Reza Shah deposed Ahmad Mirza, the last

Qajar king, and became the King of Iran, establishing the Pahlavi dynasty.

The Shah introduced many great reforms, reorganizing the Army, government administration and finance. He abolished all special rights granted to foreigners and improved transportation by building roads and the Trans-Iranian railway. He also introduced modern education and stepped up industrialization. His achievements were great, and in 1935, Persia became Iran.

However, his attempts at modernization have been criticized for being 'too fast' and 'superficial,' and his reign was considered a time of oppression, corruption, and unfair taxation, criticisms typical of police states.

During WW II, the allies protested his rapprochement with the Germans, and in 1941 British and Russia forces invaded and occupied Iran. After ruling Iran for 16 years, Reza Shah was forced to abdicate in favor of his son Mohammad Reza, and died in exile in Johannesburg, South Africa.

Mohammad Reza Shah was crowned in 1941 at the age of 21, and focused primarily on nationalization and modernization. The new young Shah initially took a very hands-off role in government and allowed Parliament to hold much of the political power.

In 1951, Prime Minister Mohammad Mosaddegh received the vote required from the Parliament to nationalize the British-owned oil industry, a situation known as the Abadan Crises. Despite British pressure, including an economic blockade, nationalization continued. Mossadegh was briefly removed from power in 1952 but was quickly re-appointed by the Shah due to a popular uprising in support of the premier, and he in turn forced the Shah into brief exile in August 1953 after a failed military coup by Imperial Guard Colonel Nematolah Nassiri.

I vividly remember military trucks and private automobiles loaded with solders and demonstrators driving up and down Chahar Bagh Avenue, Isfahan's main boulevard with slogans 'Long Live Mosaddegh,' and 'Death to the Shah.'

In the evening they attempted to pull down the statues of Reza Shah, the previous monarch, sitting gallantly on a horse and fully dressed in military uniform. For hours they hacked and sawed at the legs of the horse unsuccessfully. The next night they came back and tied the statue to a large truck and just pulled it off its stand. Both nights I was among the thousands of people shouting and enjoying the show.

I was only twelve and didn't understand what was going on, but it sure was exciting!

Shortly thereafter, on August 19, 1953, a successful coup was headed by retired army general Fazlollah Zahedi, organized by and orchestrated by the newly formed American CIA with the active support of Britain's MI6, known as Operation Ajax. The coup and propaganda campaign was designed to turn the population against Mosaddegh and remove him from office, and he was arrested and found guilty of treason. Today many Iranians remember him with anger; others with admiration for his courage and insight. His sentence was reduced to house arrest on his family estate, but his foreign minister, Hossein Fatemi, was executed. Fazlollah Zahedi succeeded him as prime minister and suppressed opposition to the Shah, specifically the National Front and Communist Tudeh Party.

It seemed like the same people driving through the streets of the city and shouting "death to the Shah" a few nights earlier had reversed course with a new slogan, "long live the Shah!"

It was like an eternity had passed since that day on the bridge when I barely escaped the police on the back of Hamand's bicycle.

In the meantime, the statue of Reza Shah was returned to its original pedestal, only reinforced to make future attempts more difficult. The Shah apparently had a grand time in Rome while in exile for several days, wining and dining with celebrities, including Gina Lollobrigida, the sexy Italian movie star. As they say, it's good to be the king.

As long as you reinforce your statue.

Shortly after the Shah's return to power, the government of Iran signed a pact with the U.S. as part of President Truman's 'Point Four Program,' calling for the United States to provide basic needs and supplies to build up the Iranian economy. For some reason the Tudeh Party was opposed to this and began street demonstrations in protest. One day when Hamand and I were riding our bicycles, we happened to be passing the '4 Points' headquarters in Isfahan. I don't know why, but out of the blue Hamand shouted, "Death to the U.S. and their 4 Points!"

Suddenly a group of men ran outside and started chasing us. Hamand peddled hard and got away, but they grabbed me and took me inside. I was terrified. I was only 15, but I knew what these men were capable of.

"Why did you shout those words?"

"I don't know."

"Why?!"

"It wasn't me! It was my friend!"

I was seated in an uncomfortable wooden chair, surrounded by angry men with ominous faces. They began my interrogation in earnest, becoming increasingly aggressive. Horrible thoughts roiled my mind, and I truly believed I might never see my home again.

I burst into tears.

"I don't know about Tudeh Party! I'm only fifteen!"

I was really bawling now, and finally, under intense pressure, I broke down and blamed it all on Hamand. Frankly, I never had inclination toward any political party and was just too young to care. The men looked skeptical, but fortunately one of the men vouched for me since he knew my father, and finally they let me go. I had just gotten my first real taste of Iranian politics, and I didn't like it one bit.

My parents never found out about this incident.

During my teenage years, I would typically go out most evenings with friends and prowl the streets looking for mischief. One of our chief amusements was to find a religious Mullah riding his donkey. One of us would sneak up behind him and shove a cornhusk up the animal's ass. The inevitable violent reaction of the ass' ass would usually result in the Mullah being thrown into the air and onto the street, his turban rolling down the lane. We would laugh ourselves silly at the thought of the Mullah attempting to extricate the offending husk.

It was even more thrilling when we could afford to get drunk on cheap wine or vodka.

One of my friends who lived around the corner had a very strict Moslem father who insisted that all the members of his family fast during the holy month of Ramadan. My friend, however, did not prescribe to that, and every day at lunchtime he would come to my house and stuff himself. Once he had gone home and burped in front of his father, who demanded to know why his son was belching during a fast.

At least he didn't fart.

One evening my mother took my sister and me to the theatre in Isfahan. We had two theatres and three cinemas in Isfahan at that time. During the second act, some men in the audience stood up all of a sudden and started shouting and bad-mouthing the play, claiming the comedy was not appropriate for an Islamic society. Suddenly the curtains dropped and everyone stampeded for the exits. When we made it outside, we witnessed a mass demonstration with thousands marching down Chaharabagh Avenue carrying signs and banners with Islamic slogans.

The crowd whipped itself into a frenzied state, and people began to attack and vandalize all the liquor stores, smashing windows and breaking bottles of booze on the sidewalk. Within hours, the gutters were flowing with alcohol. The streets smelled for days.

The liquor stores stayed closed for a few months, but gradually they all reopened and everything went back to normal.

At least for a time.

Hamand's father, Dr. Biati, was well known in Isfahan and beyond for his generosity, as well as his services. Peasants from the surrounding villages would all come and sit outside his house where he saw patients, forming long lines to see him, often waiting for hours. Many brought live chickens or sheep, eggs, or whatever they had to barter for his services. The doctor would never turn anyone away, even if they had nothing to offer him. Many nights I would get a call from Hamand, informing me that his father has been summoned to a remote village to visit a critical patient and asking if I would accompany him and his father.

They would pick me up in their WWII vintage Willys jeep, often after midnight, with Hamand and I sitting on the rear metal seats. The chauffeur would often drive for several hours on rough gravel roads until we reached the village covered in dust.

Upon arrival, usually in the wee hours of the morning, a small welcoming committee would greet us and show us to our beds, usually a pillow and blanket on the floor of a nearby home. In the morning we ate organic eggs and freshly baked bread, along with delicious cheese and butter for breakfast while the patient was attended to. The doctor would join us afterwards, and when we left, the villagers would shower him with gifts of produce or meat or whatever they had, which he would rarely accept because he felt they needed it more than he did.

He was a true gentleman, generous of heart and spirit, and a credit to his profession.

When I was 14, my mother took me to Dr. Biati to have my tonsils checked. Upon arrival in his office he sat me down in a rather forbidding chair and asked me to open my mouth. I could not help but notice that he was holding a vicious-looking instrument in his hand.

I pulled away suspiciously. "What's that?" I asked.

"It's merely to measure the size of your tonsils, Ahmad. Now relax and open up, eh?"

I did, and he swiftly reached in my mouth and casually clipped one of my tonsils without any anesthetics. I felt blood in my throat, and while I sat there in stunned silence, he clipped the other just as quickly. With blood pouring from my mouth, he smiled and guided me to my feet.

"Eat lots of ice cream for the next three days," he said, and nodded to my mother as she took my arm and walked me out the door. The removal took all of two minutes.

A few days later Hamand shows up at my house proudly showing off his new orange color bicycle that his father had just bought him. He kept riding around, making everyone envious.

I asked my father to buy me a bike also but he refused. Finally after months of nagging and keeping up the pressure, he relented and bought me a green bike. I was so enthralled I could not stop looking at my bike. I even kept it next to my bed and dreamed about it most nights.

One day I rode my bike to high school to show it to my classmates and left it on the bike rack along with all the other bikes. After class I went to ride it home and it was gone, stolen. I was so heartbroken I could not eat or sleep for days and felt the loss as much as the drowning of my younger sister.

Since the Biati brothers were hunters, they were in the habit of re-loading their spent brass casing with #4 pellets whenever they could afford to buy it, and if not they would substitute lentil seeds for pellets.

Once when I was 16, I went to their house on Norouz day to wish them a happy New Year. They were entertaining a large number of family and friends for the holiday, and invited me inside. The older guests were in one room and the rest of us, some twelve youngsters, were sitting on the floor in another, chatting and having a good time. It was then that Narand, Hamand's older brother, decided was a good a time to re-load his 12 gauge shells for future hunts.

I was given the responsibility of pulling out the spent-primer, using an instrument that first punched a hole in the primer, then pulled it out. As I was routinely pulling them out, one of the shells exploded and discharged the pellets inside. Apparently the shell had not gone off when fired. Basand, the oldest brother, who was sitting across the room, screamed and grabbed his left thigh, which was bleeding profusely. His father, who was entertaining the elderly guests in the next room, rushed in when he heard the explosion, followed by screams. Being a doctor, he immediately took steps to stop the bleeding and quickly bandaged Basand's thigh.

Meanwhile, I went out to the courtyard, crying hysterically. I was beside myself, not knowing what to do. Subsequent x-rays showed that 136 pellets had embedded themselves under the skin but no permanent damage had been caused. Everyone agreed it was an accident and not my fault, but it could have easily been fatal, so we were very fortunate, indeed.

A year later Basand was drafted into the Iranian army, but was declared disabled and exempted from service due to the presence of those pellets. He somewhat cynically expressed his gratitude to me, and offered to return the favor sometime if I was interested.

I told him I'd pass.

One of the highlights of my early years was always visiting my Uncle Mostafa and his family in Tehran during the summer. I would spend a couple of weeks with his new family, where I babysat his young son, eleven years my junior, a good part of the time. He was a very bright kid and eventually grew up to be a rocket scientist in California, designing tanks and armored vehicles for the U.S. army.

During one of my annual visits, the first 'department store' in Tehran had just opened, and had everything imaginable within its walls. Ferdousi even had electric stairs! Since I had never seen such a thing I breathlessly rushed over and ran up and down the escalators for hours on end.

Even today, I have to smile and stifle the urge to run whenever I board an escalator.

During my high school years, I was preoccupied with sports and joined the school's soccer and basketball teams. I also blossomed in Ping-Pong, and in the 11th grade I became the school's Ping-Pong champion. An announcement to that affect, which included my picture, was printed in the national newspaper. Letters from all over Iran arrived, expressing interest in meeting me.

I responded to just one: From a boy about my own age living in Abadan, a southern city in Iran known for its oil refinery on the Persian Gulf.

Upon his invitation, I flew down and spent a few days at his home, meeting his family and enjoying their Southern hospitality. He took me to the local country club where I put on a Ping-Pong clinic and played some of his friends. They were an extremely nice bunch of boys and seemed to enjoy my presence and company.

A month later, I reciprocated by inviting him to my house in Isfahan where we had a good time.

I think he enjoyed our hospitality, as well. Soon after I left Iran and we lost contact, but I'll never forget our shared experience.

Basketball Team (Seated second from the right)

During that era, the American movie star James Dean had become every teenage boy's idol. Not wanting to be left out, I dressed in blue jeans and white tee shirts and even imitated his walk, just like I observed in Rebel without a Cause. During the summer of 1958, while I was visiting Tehran, a friend took me to a popular cross-junction and I was shocked to see over a hundred boys about my age all dressed like James Dean, each one trying to outdo the next fellow and all trying to impress the girls passing by.

Needless to say, I now understood there truly was only one James Dean.

In my final year of high school, I got a part in a play representing the son of a poor farmer who was critically ill. I was happy to be onstage, but my only line was to beg the doctor to save my father. The first two nights, I dressed like a poor peasant boy and played my role as well as I could, which of course pleased the director. There's probably nothing more annoying to a director than an actor playing a small part who tries to hog the spotlight.

But when I learned the third and final night's performance had been reserved exclusively for the girls' high school, I became just such an actor. I put on my James Dean outfit, greased my hair and showed up for the show. When the director saw me he was up in arms and protested my appearance, but I refused to change. I couldn't wait to get in front of that audience full of girls, and I did exactly that. I suppose I looked more like the rich doctor's son than the poor farmer's son, but I could feel the eyes of the audience on me and that made up for everything.

There may have been only one James Dean, but I had only one chance to strut my stuff and I took it.

When the school put another production on later in the year about Genghis Khan, the director would not give me a role. I guess he was worried I would dress up like Marlon Brando. But I remember watching the play the first night and not minding at all. The boy playing Genghis had a droopy mustache glued to his upper lip. One side drooped comically, which he constantly tried to blow back in place, to very little success. Between that and his ill-fitting costume, he could barely handle his sword with both hands.

I left the performance secure in the knowledge that I would have rather spoken one line as James Dean than a thousand with a saggy mustache.

As the Persian New Year approached on March 21st, the high school students would boycott classes, demanding more days off, which the principal resisted.

This tug of war went on every year for a few days with neither side yielding, and in the final analysis nothing was accomplished except the students missed a few classes.

Which, come to think of it, was the point all along.

During the 50's the movie industry in India exploded and produced movie after movie quite a few of which were exported to Iran. Their two main stars, Raj Kapoor and Narges captured the audience's attention and became extremely popular. So it became quite common for us to go to the cinema to watch the latest Indian movie starring these two characters. They even paid a visit to Iran for and were greeted by thousands of people upon their arrival at the airport.

My friend Hamand fell in love with my younger sister Shahla, who was 16 at the time. When he approached my parents and proposed marriage, they rejected him because of his young age. This infuriated him, and one night he fired a 22-caliber bullet into our front door and scrawled "the Bullet of Revenge" next to the wood before setting the door on fire, albeit with minimal damage.

The next day my father installed a metal door.

During my senior year, I became attracted to a girl who happened to be the daughter of the Isfahan police chief. There's a saying that when a boy reaches puberty, he falls in love with the first girl who looks his way. I suppose this was true in my case. She seemed somewhat attracted to me as well, but our relationship was limited mostly to shared glances on the way to school and only from a distance. On a typical day I would pretend to be studying by the river and wait for her chauffeur-driven car to go by arrive and try to casually catch her eye from afar.

Occasionally, if we happened to be in the same cinema, after the movie I might steal a few more glances and exchange a discrete smile if I got lucky, again only from a distance. After a few months of this foolishness, my sister Shahla took pity on me and arranged an invitation to a party at her friend's house where my love would also be in attendance.

There, for the first time, I was able to actually speak to her!

My heart was racing as I tried everything in my power to stay casual and appear as cool as James Dean. She seemed impossibly mature, but I think she was probably as nervous as I was. When she offered to teach me to dance the Paso Double, my heart nearly leapt from my chest.

When we touched for the first time on the dance floor, I felt warm and lightheaded. My body temperature soared and I got very excited, but this was all new to me and I did not know how to react.

Thankfully, over time I have managed to learn a few things about women since then.

Our relationship flowered after that, and whenever possible she would sneak a conversation by calling my sister, who would then chat for a moment and then hand the telephone over to me. Everything was hush-hush since boy-girl relationships prior to marriage were frowned on. During one of these conversations she mentioned that her father was planning to send her to London after high school to further her education.

My father, on the other hand, had dealt with German advisors at the factory where he worked and grown partial to that country. He even taught himself the language. He felt the Germans had superior education and industry, and had shipped my older brother Reza there a couple of years earlier, and intended to send me there as well after high school. But as soon as my girlfriend informed me she was headed for London, I insisted on England, and eventually convinced my father to send me there. My argument was that England offered a much better educational system than Germany, all in the hope of joining my girlfriend when she went there.

In reality I knew nothing about England and didn't speak a word of English.

III.
1960's

London, England

"Winds of Change"

ON OCTOBER 23, 1959, I boarded a KLM flight for Dusseldorf, Germany with a stop in Paris. I can't tell you how
excited I was to leave the country and see the world for the
first time. I was going to spend a few days with my brother
Reza in Germany before going on to London. At the Paris Airport, as soon as the airplane door was opened and the steps
lowered, a large group of reporters and photographers
stormed the plane taking pictures of a pretty young Iranian
lady who was getting off the plane. The next day her picture
was plastered across the front pages of all the Parisian papers.
I had just flown to Paris with Farah Dibba, the future wife of
the Shah of Iran, his third. She was visiting Paris to shop for
her wedding dress.

Reza picked me up at Dusseldorf airport and we drove to Krefeld, some 20 miles away, where he had rented a room in a small house occupied by his German landlady and her teenage son. He was studying chemical engineering, specializing in dyes for the textile industry.

The ten days I spent with him was a real eye-opener for me. This was my first exposure to the Western world. I will never forget going to a public spa to swim in the pool. After swimming, we went into the shower room where a bunch of young German boys were taking a shower. As soon as we walked in, they all ran out looking terrified. Reza explained that his hairy body petrified them every time. In the evenings he would take me out with his friends to meet German girls but I was too shy to even approach them. Plus I did not speak the language.

Ten days later, I flew to London not knowing what to expect, but what I found there would change my life forever.

At London's Heathrow Airport, I was met by an associate of my father, a Jewish fellow named Joo Joo, a businessman from Isfahan who I'm sure had been paid well to get me settled me in that large and confusing city.

As soon as we got into the city, I was immediately intimidated. I was not quite nineteen, and there I was in one of the largest, most cosmopolitan cities in the western world, and I didn't speak the language.

I was a long way from Isfahan.

Joo Joo took me to an inexpensive hotel on Old Cromwell Road, where he had rented a room for me temporarily. He himself lived in a rental complex around the corner from my hotel. The next morning he picked me up, took me out for breakfast and afterwards we traveled by subway to Oxford Circus and I enrolled in the London School of English on Prince St. to learn the language. Joo Joo also gave me a briefing on the use of the subway, or 'tube,' and how to commute to school every day. The school itself, which was a real melting pot of many nationalities, later assisted me in finding permanent accommodations in the form of a single room.

My tiny room had a bed, a coin operated gas stove, and nothing else. I shared a bathroom down the hall with all the other tenants. My landlady Mrs. Duran was a sweet, middle-aged English lady who was always content and jolly.

In the early days, Joo Joo pushed me to go out and meet girls both for sex and to learn the language. He suggested I go to Piccadilly Circus and ask girls out to dinner, and even taught me a line to use for this purpose.

So I took the tube to Piccadilly Circus one evening, stood on the corner, and after long deliberation I built up enough courage to approach a young woman.

"Would you like to have me for dinner?" I asked.

She reacted angrily and said something I didn't understand before walking away.

Eventually I discovered my error and had to laugh.

Soon after I settled in London I wrote to my girlfriend in Iran asking when she planned to join me. I signed the letter using a pre-arranged female name, pretending I was a classmate of hers from high school in case her parents opened her mail. After a month and a half she finally wrote back and informed me that her father had changed his mind and that she would not be coming to London after all. I was devastated. What would I do without the love of my life? She was the reason I had come to London in the first place!

But soon enough I met a beautiful red head who made me forget all about her.

When Ursula showed up one day in my English class, all of the male heads turned her way and most of the females. She was gorgeous, elegant, and more importantly, just as lonely as I was. I asked her out immediately.

She was the daughter of a major German industrialist in Nuremburg, sent to London to learn English to assist her father in his daily international business dealings, and we started seeing a lot of each other. Both of us were a long way from our family and friends, so we clung to each other.

She also took my virginity, which I was eager to give, of course. But more than that, she was also a very good teacher in bed, and so I was much the better for our relationship.

Clinging to a girl like Ursula wasn't the most unpleasant experience of my life, I can tell you.

That Christmas I took the train to Germany and joined Reza in Krefeld. His Mutti (landlady) roasted a turkey and a pork leg with all the trimmings, and we stuffed ourselves nearly to death.

Upon my return to London, I was hooking up with Ursula more and more. We'd go out quite a bit, socializing and trying to improve our English. I thought our relationship was progressing quite well, but unbeknown to me, she was also dating an Italian hairdresser. I suppose I should have known something was up because she would excuse herself and disappear regularly, but I was young and trusting. It was my first real relationship.

In July of the following year, 1960, she just disappeared. A friend of hers told me that she had been summoned by her father back to Germany. But she left without a single word of farewell, which was hard to understand and even more difficult to take. I was heartbroken, and threw myself into my studies. I was getting better with my English, and earlier in the year I had started to look into Universities to accomplish the main purpose of my presence in England, to obtain a degree. With some help from my English teacher, I composed a letter and sent it to some big name Universities like Oxford and Cambridge seeking admission to their architectural school.

Now, I should explain that when I was growing up in Iran, there were two basic professions that were regarded respectable, and they were drummed into every little boy's head. One was a doctor and the other an architect. If you were fortunate enough to be one of these respected professionals, you could ask for the hand of any girl in marriage, from any wealthy and respected family and they would happily accept. Those professions carried a lot of weight in Iranian Society.

Since I could not stand the sight of blood, I elected to pursue a career as an architect, much to my mother's dismay. She loved me and would be happy with either, but I knew she was always disappointed that none of her sons ended up being a doctor.

I received polite rejections from all the Universities I had applied to, advising me to first complete the required pre-university GCE (General Certificate of Education) levels before attempting to enter any school. Under the British Education System, a student was required to obtain an "A" (advanced) level in three specific subjects and an "O" (Ordinary) level in five before he could be considered for admission to any university. This required a two-year commitment. In my search for schools that offered GCE coverage, I came across one in Folkestone, a pretty little town on the English coast in Kent.

I took the train from London to Folkestone and was interviewed by Mr. Wheeler, the college principal. He was a charmingly chubby Englishman with a shiny bald head, rosy cheeks and a perpetually red nose.

After admitting that I was the first foreign student he ever had interviewed, he was only too delighted to accept me. After returning to London and reporting this to a bunch of Iranian students at my English school, they all promptly applied to Folkestone Tech, and Mr. Wheeler was delighted to see that his college had suddenly gained so much popularity and was only too happy to accept them all for GCE courses.

During the early months of my attendance at the English school in London, I became acquainted with another fellow student from Iran named Bijan, and we hit it off immediately. A couple of months later, a close friend of his from Iran also joined us at the English school and we all hung around together much of the time. A couple of weeks after his arrival, this fellow got quite horny and begged me to line up a prostitute for him. Figuring that my English was adequate for the task after being in London for only two months, he urged me to call one of ladies who advertised their services in public telephone booths by posting their picture and phone number on the walls.

So finally one day, after building up the courage, I deposited a shilling in the phone box and dialed one of the numbers. I listened to the woman at the other end without understanding a single word she said, and when it sounded as if she was asking me a question, I quickly hung up out of some irrational fear of rejection. How silly was that? She was a prostitute who advertised in phone booths. Presumably she made dates for sex without ever seeing the client. But that was what went through my head.

When I exited the phone booth, my friend was waiting anxiously.

"Well?" he demanded. "Where do I go? When can I see her?"

This guy was really horny. I knew he would never let me hear the end of it if I told him I had hung up on her.

"English prostitutes don't service foreigners," I replied, matter-of-factly.

You should have seen the look on his face. He was crushed. But at least that got him off my back. I'm sure he soon found someone, though. He was just too anxious. If anyone ever needed to get laid, it was him.

Bijan, on the other hand, got lucky right away. A few days after the phone box debacle, he picked up a girl and took her to dinner. After the meal they went to Hyde Park and went behind a bush to fool around. As they were getting it on, a policeman saw them. The Bobby coughed politely and said, "I say, the park is closing in five minutes. Could you possibly hurry it up." Typical of the British police.

A few days later, another Iranian student arrived in London for school. He was the son of a wealthy industrialist from my hometown of Isfahan. In fact, his father owned the factory where my father worked. After a few weeks in London, he just disappeared. I heard that one day while boating on the Serpentine Lake at Hyde Park, he grabbed one of the Queen's white geese and wrung its neck in order to take it back to his flat and cook it for dinner. Being mid-afternoon with hundreds of witnesses, he was arrested and deported promptly from the country.

During the summer of 1960, before moving to Folkestone to start my GCE courses, I paid another visit to my brother Reza in Germany. A few days after my arrival in Krefeld, we got into his 1952 VW and drove some 220 km. south to the city of Heidelberg where Reza was scheduled to take his Toffel exam the next morning to qualify to go to the U.S. to complete his post-graduate degree at Lowell University in Massachusetts.

After we arrived in Heidelberg that evening, we bought two six-packs of beer and looked for a cheap hotel to spend the night. Much to our disappointment, there were no vacancies, so we just drank all the beer and passed out in the car outside the exam center. By the time we woke up it was past 11:00 AM and the exam was over. Reza didn't however seem that disappointed and suggested we drive to Holland for some sightseeing before heading to England.

On the way home we spent the night at Baden-Baden in Germany and Reza took me to the casino there. Being my first time, I was overwhelmed and in total awe. The grandness of that majestic establishment was almost beyond my comprehension. Reza was fond of playing roulette and explained the rules before giving me a single Deutsch Mark, which I placed on the number 14, my date of birth. Unbelievably, 14 came up and paid 35 Marks.

I was beside myself. Although I gave some of it back, it blew my mind how easily money could be won and lost in a casino.

In my later career, I often reflected back on my first real experience with true capitalism.

Having come from a Muslim background, I found Europe with its history and culture totally fascinating. We spent a day touring Amsterdam, then drove to the coastal town of Ostend in Belgium and took a ferry to Dover, England. After spending a few days with me in London, Reza drove back to Germany to continue his schooling.

In August of 1960, I moved to Folkestone and rented a room in a house owned by a redheaded Irishman and his feisty Italian wife, a hard-working woman who run that household with an iron fist. Soon after my arrival, Bijan and another Iranian student who had followed me to Folkestone Technical College also rented rooms in that same house.

Shortly after moving to Folkestone, Bijan and I each bought a Vespa Scooter on credit and started cruising and exploring the coastal areas near Folkestone.

On my Vespa in Folkestone

As classes began in September of 1960 and I got a look at the textbooks, I realized how limited my grasp of the English language was. All the technical terms seemed so foreign to me. So with an English-Iranian dictionary in one hand and my textbook in the other, I started the laborious task of educating myself in physics, chemistry and mathematics.

It was slow and arduous work at first, but since that was the sole purpose of me being in England, I put my foot down and spent endless hours studying my chosen objects. Words like 'magnitude,' 'differentiation,' 'equilibrium,' and 'isosceles' seemed like they were from a different planet, but soon I began to slowly master the texts, and I quickly moved up to the top of my class.

Across the street from our college was located a girl's college, and every lunchtime all the girls would walk over and share the same cafeteria with us. For the Iranian boys, it was like spending an hour every day in paradise, and we would wait anxiously for lunchtime to arrive so we could mingle and chat with the girls. For the ten Iranian students, it was like turning a bunch of hungry young lions loose on a group of delicate gazelles; we salivated at the mere sight of them. Most of us put our studies on the back burner and started chasing the girls.

The college soon initiated a Sunday get-together called International Evening where the boys and girls could listen to music, dance, play Ping-Pong, watch "Danger Man" starring Patrick McGoohan on telly, and just have a good time. The only bad thing was that there was no alcohol allowed. This was the Principal's idea of exposing foreign students to British culture, and let me tell you, we all wanted some exposure.

I started dating a pretty blond with a thick cockney accent named Carol. We went out for a while until she abruptly broke off the relationship without any explanation. So I started dating a 17 year-old English-Italian brunette named Toni. Her real name was Elizabeth and she was a real spitfire. Some 25 years later, long after we had been married, I learned that she had paid Carol two-and-a-half shillings to stay away from me so she could have me all for herself. In other words, she had bought me out for the cost of a phone call.

I'd say we both got a pretty good deal.

As the 1960 Christmas holiday approached, Bijan and I decided to ride my Vespa scooter to Germany. I would be visiting my brother Reza in Krefeld, while Bijan was going to spend Christmas with his uncle in Hanover. As we were crossing Belgium on a bitterly cold day, Bijan lost control of the bike and we crashed into the asphalt. Fortunately it all happened in mid-afternoon near some houses, and a woman rushed out, took us inside her house and called a nearby doctor, who soon arrived in a fancy Cadillac. I could see why my mother wanted a doctor in the family.

He bandaged my right leg, which had lost a good bit of skin on the asphalt, plus other assorted minor bruises. Bijan was also bandaged, and the lady of the house gave us coffee and cookies. After a few hours, we were once again on our way. They both were most kind and would not accept any compensation for their hospitality and services rendered.

For minor traffic mishaps, I highly recommend the area, especially during the holidays.

Bandaged like two Egyptian Mummies, we reached Krefeld near midnight, and the next day Bijan took the train to Hanover to visit his uncle.

A couple of days after Christmas, I asked an old friend from Isfahan named Bahram, who was also studying in Krefeld, if he would ride on the back of my scooter with me to Nuremberg. I wanted to see Ursula, the sexy German girl who had deserted me a few months earlier.

As it happened, my old friend Hamand and his older brother Narand were living in Nuremberg at the time, so we planned to stay with them for the duration.

It was raining hard the day we had planned to depart, so we waited all day for it to stop, but by midnight, with no letup in sight, we decided to leave anyway and started on our 250 km journey. We drove down the Autobahn in the pouring rain for seven hours, and the only incident en-route was when traffic came to a sudden stop and we ran into the back of the car in front of us. Fortunately there was no damage or injury, and we reached Nuremberg just after sunrise.

Hamand and his brother warmly received us, and exhausted, we slept that whole day and into the night. The next morning, Bahram and I were dropped off outside a high-rise apartment complex where Ursula lived on the 20th floor.

I rang the bell and her mother opened the door. After I introduced myself, she called Ursula, who walked over in her bathrobe looking completely shocked to see me there. But they received us quite pleasantly and invited us to stay for coffee and cake. While I was sitting there, I noticed a small carpet that I had personally woven for her hanging on the wall, which portrayed a scene on the high seas.

As we were leaving, Ursula invited me to join her and her family for a luncheon on Sunday at her father's country club, which I happily accepted. She picked me up in a new Fiat her father had just bought for her, and drove me to a beautiful country club on the outskirts of Nuremberg. There, she introduced me to her father and other family members and we had a pleasant lunch.

After lunch, her father pulled me aside, and in a polite German businesslike fashion, made it abundantly clear that I should forget about Ursula and return to London and mind my own business. He hinted that he had already lined up a young man who happened to be the son of a German business associate for Ursula to marry.

I found it ironic that marriages were arranged in the west just like back in my parents' day. The cultures were not so different in many ways.

I said my thanks and bade farewell to all of them, and Ursula dropped me off at Hamand's apartment with a nice goodbye kiss that told me she might not go along with her father's plans, but unfortunately I never found out.

After a couple of days, Bahram and I got on my scooter and drove back to Krefeld on a nice sunny day without any incidents. Bijan re-joined me there and we started our journey back to England. By the time we reached Ostend on the Belgian coast, it was late in the day and the last ferry had already left. Not being able to afford a night at a hotel, Bijan just hung around the scooter while I tried to get some sleep under a fishing boat, which was lying upside down on the beach. It was extremely cold, and the wind howled constantly, keeping me awake most of the night. We caught the first ferry the next morning and sailed back to Dover, England, and then drove back to Folkestone.

As the summer of 1961 approached, Bijan and I started looking for summer jobs. We'd heard that working the Dover docks unloading freight was good pay, so every morning we would get up very early and ride our scooters the eight miles by 5 AM to get in line for job selection. This was the routine we followed every day. We worked till noon, collected our wages, and drove back. We mostly unloaded produce like potatoes or tomatoes from cargo ships. It was hard work but good money. Most of our coworkers were Irish or from Yorkshire, and they all went to the pubs after collecting their paychecks and drunk their wages.

In August of 1961 I received a letter from my friend Bahram in Germany inviting me to join him on a drive to Iran. Apparently, a fellow Iranian student originally from Isfahan was planning to drive his 1952 Mercedes 220 all the way from Krefeld to Iran some 2850 miles away and I was welcome to join them. I was feeling a little homesick, so I elected to go along. I took the train to Krefeld and a couple of days later the four of us piled into his black Mercedes and started the long journey. The fourth person was another student from Isfahan, also homesick for his family and friends.

Unbeknown to me, the owner of the car turned out to be a nutcase who insisted on driving fast and reckless 24 hours a day. He would overtake cars and trucks on any part of a road, regardless of the conditions, even running oncoming cars off the road if they were to get in his way. We arrived in Turkey after 58 hours of nonstop driving. While crossing the country, he finally stopped the car in city of Kayseri and parked it in the main square. He then opened a suitcase full of sunglasses and started selling them. Before long, we were surrounded by a large crowd of men who started snapping up the merchandise at hefty prices. Before long, the bidding and shouting started to get out of control, and we packed and quickly left. This was obviously not a new situation for the driver. We stopped for a quick wash by a trough and headed east towards Iran.

We reached the Iranian border the next day and continued to Tabriz, which was the closest large city. There we checked into a cheap motel to clean up and spend the night. We planned to drive to Tehran the next day. However, the next

Washing by the trough in Turkey

morning when we all showed up for breakfast the owner of the car informed us that he had found a buyer for his Mercedes and sold it at a great profit, and offered to buy us train ticket to complete the last leg of our journey.

That particular model Mercedes 220 was extremely popular and desirable for taxi use, and it had been his intention all along to turn this into a profitable drive, a fact he had neglected to mention until after the fact. I was actually relieved to take the train the rest of the way since his driving was so reckless, and after spending a couple of weeks in Iran, I flew back to London.

I decided then never to take such a long trip in a car, but that was a promise meant to be broken.

One of my classmates at Folkestone Tech was a young English fellow named Tim. During my second year I rented a room in his house, which was located in Sandgate, a small seacoast village about five miles from Folkestone. It was a charming little house, and his cheerful mother cooked me breakfast and dinner every day, which freed up more time for me to focus on my studies. Tim and his mother were very close since his father had passed away when Tim was a boy. They also had an Alsatian dog named Lassie, which rounded out the family, you might see.

Like a lot of the students, I was always looking for ways to earn money. Over Christmas of 1961, I secured a part-time job at the local post office delivering packages in an over-loaded truck with two English fellows. At the same time, I was also working part-time as figure model at the Folkestone art school. I would sit on a stool in my swimsuit and pose for the life-drawing classes. I would hold my position for twenty-five minutes at a time, but my eyes were free to roam, and I have to admit I enjoyed looking at the pretty girls in the classes. On the breaks between poses, all the female students would congregate around the model stand and flirt with me.

Like they say, the money wasn't much but the fringe benefits were excellent.

I spent Christmas Day with my girlfriend Elizabeth and her foster parents John and Betty, to whom she referred as her aunt and uncle. They lived in the army barracks in Hythe, a quaint coastal village about eight miles south of Folkestone in a house provided by the British Army. They had a large, beautiful Siberian Husky named Tina. Elizabeth's real mother was also there. She was a high-class call girl in London, so I guess you can understand why Elizabeth lived with her foster parents.

It was quite an experience. The entire day is still etched in my memory. I was utterly overwhelmed by the English Christmas traditions, what with crackers and paper crowns and balloons to be popped. It was also my first exposure to real English cooking, with roast turkey, ham, beef, Yorkshire pudding, and mince pie for dessert. Quite different from what I was used to, food and otherwise. It was a great day to be with Elizabeth and her family. I felt very close to her and really enjoyed the experience.

One interesting memory had nothing at all to do with the meal or family, however. I remember going to the bathroom and seeing the words "Government Property" stamped on all the toilet paper, which I found hilarious. Uncle John worked for the British army.

In the spring of 1961, Bijan and I sold our Vespa scooters and bought Minis on credit. Mine was white and his was maroon. I loved zipping around in that car. There's something about a little sports car that really whets your appetite for speed, which is always fun.

One evening I was driving Elizabeth home along the coastal road, and the sea was really rough. Huge swells were violently crashing against the seawall, and a huge wave rose up and smacked my Mini like a flyswatter, causing the car to stall.

We were on a particularly desolate stretch of road and basically just sat there waiting for someone to come by, because the car simply would not start. No one did, but after a couple of hours the Mini finally dried out enough to start, and I really put the pedal down to get her home.

There were no cell phones back then, of course, and we didn't even pass any payphones. It was every young man's nightmare: Bringing a girl home late, facing the wrath of her parents, and not even getting laid to show for it.

Uncle John was waiting outside the front door when we pulled up. I was worried that he was going to be angry with me, but he spoke only to Elizabeth, completely ignoring me as he chastised her. That was worse than if he'd yelled at me. I would have much rather taken the brunt of his anger, but it was as if I wasn't there.

From then on I made sure to have her home on time.

During my second year at Folkestone Technical College, my mathematics teacher introduced the class to a mechanical calculator. It was a wondrous device, and we were endlessly fascinated. Its calculations required laborious operations, including rotating a handle to add, subtract, and multiply, but it was something none of us had ever seen before. I was totally enamored of this unique invention, and my mastery of the device would lead me to great heights after graduation.

In June of 1962, after completing my GCE at Folkestone, I landed a job at cleaning toilets. Not exactly what I had been hoping for, but a job was a job. I worked the night janitorial shift at Bachelore's Pea Factory near Maidstone, some 25 miles away. Irrespective of my prowess with a calculator, my tools were now a bucket and a mop, 7 nights a week. During the last couple of hours of my nightly shift, I would help in the cafeteria preparing tea and breakfast for the employees.

Around that time Bijan and I moved out of our lodgings and lived in a small tent we set up in a beautiful spot along the sea called 'Little Switzerland.' Bijan had secured a job at Dungeness Power Plant during the day, and for two months, due to our opposite work schedules, we never saw each other once even though we shared a single, tiny tent.

Before moving out of our lodgings, Bijan picked up a girl one evening and after dinner, he had driven his Mini automobile back to the beach. They were lying across the back seat kissing, and were so involved in their passion that they failed to notice the tide was rising until the water literally lapped at their seat cushions. He'd parked his car on a sloped section of beach facing the ocean, and the entire engine had been submerged in salt water. Naturally, it wouldn't start.

Bijan had had no choice but to abandon the vehicle to the sea. Talk about a cruel mistress.

The next morning, Bijan was woken up at 7:30 AM by an English policeman, who politely informed him that his car had been fished out of the sea, and the fishermen wanted an explanation. After Bijan got himself together, the sympathetic policeman drove him to where the Mini had been towed, but it was beyond repair.

The car was written off as a total loss, but at least he had a good time and his premiums were paid-to-date. You might say the insurance company paid for a very expensive lay.

When I completed my courses at Folkestone, I obtained the necessary 'A' and 'O' levels to qualify for university admission. I had worked very hard, and out of all the Iranian students who followed me there, I was the only one who accomplished that task in just two years. Ironically, one of the O level subjects acceptable was Farsi, the Iranian language, but Bijan and I were the only ones who managed to pass it.

Talking to one of my professors about my interest in Architecture, I learned for the first time that there was another aspect of building design I had not previously considered. Civil engineering dealt primarily with the technical side of buildings, and my instructor felt it was more suited to my talents. Before that moment, I was not even aware of such science, but it was going to change my life.

As I've said, boys growing up in Iran were groomed to become either doctors or architects. I think being such an ancient civilization gives us a healthy respect for the building blocks of an empire. I applied to several universities that offered degrees in Civil Engineering, and because of my grades, I was accepted by all of them. Needless to say, both my parents and I were quite proud and excited. After interviewing a handful of schools, I selected London University.

I moved to London in September 1962 to start my schooling, followed by my girlfriend Elizabeth, who secured a job with a literary agency in Soho. She shared a two bedroom flat with three other girls right across from the British Museum in central London. It was an exciting time for both of us.

I felt like I was on top of the world. It was as if my future was laid out in front of me like a wide, never-ending highway. I didn't know exactly where it went, but I sensed I was going to have quite a journey along the way there.

In the meantime, my brother Reza had completed his studies and received a degree in Chemical Engineering. He moved back to Iran and started a job in Tehran with Beyer, the giant German chemical company. My parents were extremely pleased their eldest sons were doing well, and especially happy to have Reza back in Iran.

My friend Bijan was admitted to a Provincial College in London to study for his architectural degree.

After freshman year, I got a summer job with the giant English construction firm of John Mowlem, assisting with the building of the new township of Stevenage, just north of London. It was labeled as Britain's first "New Town," and my primary responsibility was to mark the layout of the houses, streets and malls before the construction crew moved in to excavate for the foundations. It was a gratifying experience to be part of such a large, exciting project, and it gave me a fresh insight into the practical side of the science I had elected to make my career.

It wasn't modeling for college girls, but it paid a lot more.

In the meantime, Bijan had gone to Iran for a visit, and left his brand new red MG Midget in my care for the summer. While he was gone, he asked me to take the car to his girl-friend's nineteen year-old brother, who worked as a mechanic, for a tune-up.

It was a beautiful Saturday morning, and the kid took a quick look at the car and decided the engine needed to be de-coked. He quickly took the engine apart and cleaned all the valves of any carbon residue. After putting it all back together, we looked at each other and smiled. We both we thinking the same thing: That car needed to be driven! We took the car for a test drive through the busy streets of London. I was having a great time. Her brother drove like a madman, weaving in and out of traffic, and the car handled beautifully.

Until he smashed into another car.

I was glad I wasn't the one driving, thinking that Bijan as going to be furious, but the kid didn't seem worried at all, even though the left front fender was badly dented. He pulled it out using only his hands and we limped back to his work-shop. He went right to work, and within hours it all fixed and painted as if nothing had happened.

In July of 1963, Reza contacted me from Iran and asked if I could purchase a used Opel in Germany and drive it to Iran for him. Having made that trip two years earlier, I felt com-fortable undertaking the challenge and asked Elizabeth if she cared to join me. She quickly agreed and the adventure was on.

We planned to hook up with my old friend Bahram in Germany to seek his assistance in finding the car Reza wanted, but the trip was long and tiresome. First, we had to take a train from London, disembark in Dover, take a four-hour ferry across the English Channel to the Belgian port of Ostend, hop a train to Brussels, change trains and head to Dusseldorf, where we would catch our final train to Krefeld.

And that was before we drove the car to Iran!

As our train was approaching the border, a couple of German immigration officers walked through the compartments checking passports, and when they got to mine, they both just shook their heads and said, "Nicht gut."

Not good? I had an Iranian passport and a German visa, what could be wrong? But they didn't speak any English and couldn't explain the nature of the problem. I was totally baffled, and pretty worried as well. What if they didn't let me proceed? After the long, tedious trip would I actually be sent back home?

They kept my passport and when the train reached Dusseldorf that night, after they took me to an office and left me there. I told Elizabeth to keep going and take the next train to Krefeld as planned where Bahram would be waiting at the station. She was a little nervous about traveling alone, not to mention she'd never met him before, but I gave her a full description and convinced her it was the best thing.

After a long wait, a German officer who spoke limited English finally came and explained that under new orders by the Shah of Iran, every Iranian who entered Germany was required to obtain an endorsement in form of a stamp in their passport from the Iranian government permitting such an entry. No explanation was given for the reason and it was the weirdest thing I had ever come across in my travels.

A couple of hours later, they put me on an overnight train and sent me back to Brussels to visit my consulate and secure the required permit. I was so worked up with all this uncertainty that I couldn't sleep on the train, and when the train reached Brussels at five in the morning I got directions and walked the three miles to the Iranian Embassy, which didn't open for two hours.

I presented my case, they stamped my passport, and I took the next train back to Dusseldorf. I changed trains and reached Krefeld dead tired in time to join Elizabeth and Bahram for dinner. It was so good to finally be off the train, but I was so exhausted I nearly fell asleep at the table.

The next day we contacted the same Iranian fellow who'd driven us to Iran in his Mercedes two years earlier and asked for help locating a good used Opel for Reza. He not only agreed to help us find a car, but offered to help with the drive as well.

At least this time he wouldn't be able to sell the car out from under us.

It took us two weeks to find the right car, and we ended up buying a white '61 Opel from a dealer. But when we went to pick up the car the next day, the dealer told us that he had had a minor accident in the car the night before and needed to repair the damage. He sure wasn't the mechanic Bijan's girlfriend's brother was. It took this guy three days to straighten the right fender of the Opel and repaint it, after which we picked up the car for the long drive to Tehran.

The four of us, Eliza, Bahram, and our old driver friend loaded our bags on the roof rack and left Krefeld on a beautiful sunny day in early August. Just like the previous trip, we drove hard, and our only stops were for gas, food and one quick wash in a stream in Yugoslavia.

Stop for a quick lunch in Turkey

We covered the 2850-mile trip in four days and reached Tehran safely, but very tired and dusty. When we delivered the car to Reza, he introduced us to his pretty fiancé, Houri.

We spent a couple of weeks in Isfahan, where I introduced Eliza to my family and all friends. It made me feel proud to have a beautiful girl on my arm to show off. One day the two of us went shopping for antiques at the famous Bazaar of Isfahan. At a pottery store, we struck up a conversation with the owner, who was beating a copper pot into shape. When we asked him if he had any old copper works, he directed us to the back of the store and said, "All the junk is there."

Eliza and I spent a long time sifting through the 'junk,' and found some wonderful old pots and pans, which we bought for a song. The owner was only too glad to get rid of them. He could not see the value in the beautiful old things right under his nose. We had everything packed and shipped to London.

For our return journey we decided to take the bus from Tehran to Munich, which was a six-day trip. I was looking forward to a nice, relaxing trip, but as soon as we crossed into Turkey, Eliza got violently ill with a high fever and nausea. Fortunately, a medical intern was traveling with us on the bus, and he attended to her. Under the circumstances, he did his best with what limited medication he carried to stabilize her.

By the time we reached Germany, Eliza was quite weak and had lost a lot of weight, but her stomach flu eventually subsided. Still, it was a miserable trip for her. To make matters worse, when we first got to Munich, the bus had to go under a fairly low bridge, and with all the baggage on the roof rack, the driver misjudged the height and the smashed bags were thrown all over the road. We had to stop and collect our bags, some of which had opened and strewn their contents across the road. It really turned into the trip from hell, but it was also a bonding experience for Eliza and me. There's something about an adversity-filled road trip. When bad things happen and there's nowhere to go, you have to deal with each other and get through it together.

After gathering the bags and transferring them inside the bus, we continued into Munich where we all disembarked. As it happened, my old Isfahani friend Hamand had moved to Munich, and was living with another old friend who owned a gunsmith in Isfahan. They were kind enough to put Eliza and me up for a couple of nights, after which we all piled into Hamand's VW and drove to England.

We dropped Eliza off at her foster parents' in Hythe and then drove to London to my flat. Hamand and our mutual friend stayed with me for a few days before driving back to Germany. We had a great time catching up. Hamand was the kind of friend who I could go without seeing for ten years and pick up again like I'd seen him yesterday.

My second year at the university was fairly uneventful. I remained the top student in my class of twenty-four, half of who were also foreigners from countries like Spain, Nigeria, and Iraq. The other half were British.

One of my classmates was a tall blonde Englishman who was addicted to dog racing. Every day, he would walk into the classroom with a newspaper under his arm and after class he would sit down and focus on that day's dog racing and place bets on them.

One day he asked if I would like to accompany him to the track, and of course I accepted. He suggested I place a bet to make it more interesting. I walked up to the betting window and asked to place one British Pound, which was a lot of money out of my student budget. The man asked if I wanted a 'win' or 'place.' Since I did not have a clue as to what he was talking about, I asked him to explain.

"A win bet means your bet predicts the winner. A place bet predicts the winning order of the first *and* second dog."

I bet on two random dogs to finish first and second, and to my utter disbelief they came in as I predicted and I won 12 pounds! Just as in Baden-Baden, I gave much of it back with subsequent bets, but the experience definitely had an impact on my attitude towards economics. That day was the extent of my experience in dog race betting, but my friend Ron made it his side profession throughout his college years.

The following summer, in 1964, I re-joined the construction firm of John Mowlem and assisted in the construction of new runways at Heathrow Airport. It was not as interesting as the previous summer, but the experience was still valuable to my development in the field.

During my final year, we all made a field trip to Gloucestershire to explore the geological sites and learn about different rock formations. Studying the work of the greatest architect of all as found in nature was both inspiring and humbling, and I enjoyed our exploration quite a bit. The basic principles of architectural study and design are all around us all the time. Nature is a great teacher of all things.

During my freshman year in college, I began taking judo classes. Judo is all about balance, flexibility, and discipline, which are qualities valuable to anyone at any age, but in particular to young people. Today's college students would do well to study such a discipline given the wealth of distractions constantly bombarding them. Even forty years ago, Judo was of great benefit to me in that regard. By the time I was a senior, I had earned a black belt. I also loved Ping-Pong, and entered every competition I could. Eventually I became the college champion.

Anything worth doing is worth doing well, and my dedication to those pursuits paid off not only in life experiences, but also in learning. The lessons of both Judo and Ping-Pong have stayed with me my entire life. Hard work and dedication is rewarded, and there's nothing like doing something you love.

If I could have made a living playing Ping-Pong, now that would have really been something.

Everything then was to be experienced to the fullest extent. I was drinking in life as quickly as I could, and nothing seemed out of reach. That is the benefit of youth. I had unlimited optimism. I was the fearlessness of youth personified.

But few come from my homeland without being touched by tragedy, and the experience of my lost sister stayed with me. I had seen at an early age how fragile we all are, and always in the back of my mind was the knowledge that everything could change in an instant.

In June of 1965, I graduated with a high honors degree called BSC (Bachelor of Science - Civil Engineering) and shortly after that I married Eliza. I think I had known from the moment we met that we would be together. Even today, when I look in her eyes I can still see the teenage spitfire who paid her friend to take a hike so she could have me all for herself. Eliza knew exactly what she wanted and got it, and she's been a source of inspiration to me ever since.

Graduation

Our wedding took place at a church she chose in Hythe. I was required to convert to Methodism for the privilege, which I did. But that wasn't the only requirement. The priest also charged me thirty-five pounds to perform the conversion!

That's what I call effective proselyting.

I was incredibly hung over for my wedding. The night before I drank copious amounts of alcohol at my bachelor party, helped in no small way by my brother Reza, who seemed to take particular delight in my misery the next day, as was his duty as my older brother.

Not only was I feeling terrible on the inside, I didn't look all that good on the outside, either. Ironically, I had ordered a tailor-made suit for my wedding because I wanted to look especially sharp, but it was delivered just before the ceremony and was not particularly well made. One sleeve was longer than the other and the pants were too short, and there was no time to fix it.

So because I wanted to look like James Bond, I instead resembled a cross between Norman Wisdom and Pee-Wee Herman.

Eliza, as all brides, was absolutely beautiful.

My Church Wedding to Elizabeth

Right after the reception, Eliza and I drove my 1956 VW across Europe for our honeymoon. My brother Reza and his wife Houri decided to keep us company.

In their own vehicle, of course!

We took the ferry from Dover to Calais, France, which is the shortest crossing of the Channel. Calais is known as "the most English town in France," which can be taken as an insult or a compliment, depending on your allegiance.

We drove directly to Nice, a beautiful city on the Mediterranean coast in the south of France. The city isn't far from Cannes, where the famous film festival is held once a year. We laid in the sun and swam in the ocean and generally had a wonderful time. The food, the company, and the atmosphere could not have been better.

I highly recommend taking close relatives on your honeymoon. As long as you take separate cars.

After a few days there, we continued on to Italy where Reza and Houri said farewell and drove their vehicle back to Iran while Eliza and I slowly worked our way back to England. Shortly after our return, I got a job in London and started working for a civil engineering firm near Victoria Station. Every day I would take the tube to work and enjoy an Indian meal at lunch using the two and six (2.6 shilling) luncheon voucher provided by my employer as a fringe benefit. Life was good.

In May of 1966, Eliza and I went to the U.S. Embassy in Grosvenor Square in London to apply for immigration to the United States. A sour-faced woman at the front desk told us to fill out the necessary forms and we would be put on the waiting list.

"How long is the list?" I asked.

"Twenty-four years."

We could scarcely believe our ears. Twenty-four years was the minimum wait? That was a lifetime.

We were so disillusioned we didn't even bother filling out the application forms. As we walked out, we saw Canada's red and white flag flapping in the breeze across the square, so we decided to check with the Canadian embassy. We walked in and made the same request, and the reaction was the opposite of what we had experienced at the U.S. Embassy. They received us warmly and with open arms, informing us that Canada was in need of qualified civil engineers, and offered to arrange an interview with a Montréal based firm that was interviewing in London the following week!

Our timing could not possibly have been better. Within days we had our Canadian immigration visas, and when I went for the job interview with Montreal Engineering Company, I was hired on the spot. They even paid our way and arranged to pack and ship all our personal affects to Montreal at their own expense.

Once again I was struck by life's little twists and turns. Had we not noticed the flag flapping in the breeze across the square as we left the U.S. Embassy that day, we may have never thought to try the Canadian embassy.

Perhaps the wind itself had changed our lives.

In June 1966, Elizabeth and I boarded BOAC (British Overseas Aircraft Cooperation) and left London for Montreal to begin a whole new chapter in our lives.

We were met at the airport by a representative from Montreal Engineering and ushered to a beautiful downtown hotel. Within a few days we found a one-bedroom apartment in LaSalle, a suburb of Montreal from where I would take a bus to work. My job was located in downtown Montreal near Place De Arms.

We both found Montreal to be a lovely city, with its European-style architecture and diverse culture.

Elizabeth secured a job as a secretary in a brewery, and most days she would smuggle a bottle of beer in her handbag and bring it home for me. There's an old joke about the characteristics of the ideal wife, and my Eliza's new position had just taken care of the last one.

Most of my colleagues were immigrants from all over the world who had made the same journey as I in order to secure a better life. Some wanted to stay, but many just wanted to work for a few years to save enough money to go back home and live comfortably. I wasn't entirely sure at the time what was in store for me along those lines, but I was happy for the time being with Eliza in my adopted country.

Our social life suffered nary a pause, and we quickly became close friends with a couple from Holland, as well as two couples from Turkey, all about our own age. There were also two single draftsmen, one from Italy and one from Portugal, who would on occasion come along with us on dinner outings.

Montreal had hard winters, but the upside of the bitter cold weather as the great skiing nearby. On weekends during the winter months, all four couples would drive up to the Laurentian Mountains to ski.

It was a first time experience for most of us, and because of our tight budget, we would not only share rental skis, but also buy just two lift tags, one of which we attached to a man's jacket, and the other to a woman's jacket. That way we could take turns going up the ski lift by swapping jackets.

As a matter of fact, money was so tight we took the side roads back and forth to the resort just to avoid paying the $1 toll on the expressway, even though it took twice as long to make the journey. Gasoline was much less expensive in those days, but I'm still not entirely sure we shouldn't have just paid the toll.

Montreal was a charming city of primarily French-speaking inhabitants. In fact, they were so prejudice that when we spoke to them in English, they would respond in French even though everyone spoke good English.

It's still a sore point with many there to this day.

Winters were quite harsh, and everyone stayed indoors if they could help it. I'll never forget one night in a particularly cold January when my wife and I went to the movies, and upon returning to our car, my hand actually froze to the door handle.

I tried to open the door and it was as if my hand had been glued to the handle. It took a while, but eventually the warmth of my hand melted the ice enough that I was able to free my hand and open the door.

With my sleeve.

Soon after establishing ourselves in Montréal, Eliza and I once again applied to immigrate to the United States. The U.S. consulate in Ottawa was much less forbidding than its London counterpart, and so was the waiting list. We were relieved to learn that our wait would only be about three years.

I suppose had we not been told such an outrageously long wait in London, we might have looked on three years as something of a long time itself, but so often in life, as in architecture, it all depends on your perspective.

During the summer of 1967, the engineering firm sent me to Gananoque Thousand Islands on the St. Lawrence Seaway to supervise the installation of a foundation for two large Turbo Diesel Generators. It was a two-month project outside the confines of the office in a beautiful area, and a nice change from my usual routine. It also indicated a healthy respect for my skills and work ethic, which I greatly appreciated. A year later I was asked to go to St. John's Newfoundland to surprise the construction of a head office for Newfoundland Power & Light. It was another feather in my cap at work and further encouragement from my superiors, which in turn inspired me to work harder.

Before relocating to St. John's, Eliza and I decided to take a two-week vacation and drove all the way down to New Orleans in our nearly-new 1965 yellow Mustang. We initially drove all the way down to New Orleans, making stops in Kentucky to visit some colorful caves along the way.

We found New Orleans to be a wonderful city, very cosmopolitan for its size and almost like a smaller version of Montreal with a little gumbo thrown in for good measure.

After New Orleans we swung east and spent a few days on the beach in Orlando where I tried surfing for the first time. I was eager to be just like one of those characters the Beach Boys sang about, but it turned out to be a lot harder that it sounded. I split my chin on the board almost immediately and opened up a gash the size of my middle finger underneath my chin. That put a quick end to my surfing career.

Then we drove up the eastern seaboard to New York City to visit some old friends from Isfahan, one of who was working as a gynecologist at a hospital in the Bronx. He arranged for Eliza and I to use one of the empty rooms in the hospital where we slept for two nights, saving hotel costs. As we were having breakfast with him the next morning, Eliza threw up, and it was not due to the food in the hospital's cafeteria.

"Congratulations," my friend said casually.

"Excuse me, what?" I was gathering napkins for Eliza.

"You're going to be a father."

I looked at Eliza, who didn't seem nearly as shocked as I was. We had been so careful. How could this have happened? Maybe my friend didn't know what he was talking about.

I looked from my wife to my friend *the gynecologist*.

A smile slowly formed across my wife's face, matched by my own, and I took her into my arms, tears in our eyes. We had taken every precaution so as to wait until we were ready, but there was serendipity once more, waving like a flag in the breeze.

I guess we were ready, after all.

Shortly after returning to Montreal, we packed our car and drove to St. John's, stopping for the night in Nova Scotia with our Dutch friends who were assigned to a construction project there by Montreal Engineering Company. In spite of finding Montreal exciting, I was actually looking forward to a change in scenery. I always liked to experience new places and things.

Newfoundland is a large island, somewhat isolated from the rest of Canada and is mostly occupied by fisherman. It was about as different from Montreal as London was from Isfahan. They refer to it as 'the Rock' because of its topography, which is quite rugged, rocky, and distinctly lacking in greenery.

We quickly made friends with a few fellow foreigners who had settled in St. John's in recent years. I would play soccer with them on Sundays and maybe go out for a beer or two afterwards. It was always good to unwind on the weekends because I was working very hard during the week, and the job was not without stress. It was a lot of responsibility, working with and coordinating the work of a lot of subcontractors, but I was the man in charge.

I'm proud to say that the office project was completed in ten months, ahead of schedule and under budget. But that was not what I was most proud of during that amazing time in our lives. What made me the proudest was our son Darvish, born two months before the project was completed.

Looking into the eyes of my son, I knew what all my hard work had been for. His tiny hands, his feet, it was such an incredible thing to see.

Like everyone, I had heard new parents speak of the birth of their children, but there is nothing to prepare one for the actual experience.

I thought of my father back in Iran, and for the first time I understood the breadth of his love for us. It was as if I was truly a man for the very first time.

While I was working in Montréal, I couldn't help but notice that most of my colleagues in the office spent quite a bit of time on the telephone talking to their stockbrokers in a financial terms somewhat unknown to me. It was almost like another language. Having mentioned this to my wife, she bought me a book for my next birthday on the fundamentals of investing in the stock market. By the time I finished that book, I was hooked.

I went to the library and borrowed as many books as I could find on the subject, and read them cover-to-cover. It was always the same. I would read the book at night until I fell asleep, pick it up in the morning before work, and as often as not, I would be finished before bed the next night and had started on another.

A book called "How I Made a Million in the Market," by Nickolas Darvas, was the clincher for me. The book had sold over a million copies and was out a print at the time, but it was my inspiration. I began reading the financial pages of the daily newspapers every day. The more I learned, the more fascinated and enthralled I became.

I decided to get serious. My initial focus was on penny stocks, the stocks priced under a dollar. I would pretend I had bought an amount of a particular stock and then track its progress to see what profit or loss I would have made had I actually invested.

It became a bit of an obsession, those non-existent profits. I enjoyed picking a stock that went up, but it would also bother me because the money wasn't actually going into my pocket. But I was getting pretty good at it.

After feeling somewhat comfortable with the market, I cautiously took my first step. I invested $400 in a Canadian Mining Stock selling at 85 cents a share. Every morning I would check the action on my lone investment, but very little happened for some time. It was tortuous.

Then one day, I opened the paper and saw that the price had jumped all the way up to $1.20 a share on heavy volume. I ran my finger across the page again to double check, wondering if I had made a mistake. It was true. I jumped with joy and sold it immediately, every last share. I didn't know why it had gone up and I didn't care, I was just ecstatic I had made $100 profit after commissions.

I was beside myself. I was sure I was a genius who had discovered the secret of rags to riches. I kept investing and had mixed results, but that didn't dampen my enthusiasm. I became so overconfident that I even started writing a book I was going to call, "How to Make Money in Penny Stocks."

I have to laugh about that now, as my total profits at the time probably amounted to no more than a few hundred dollars.

A few weeks before leaving St. Johns, I was driving down a side street when I saw a U.S. flag outside a small, nondescript building. On impulse, I stopped and went inside. There had been a U.S. naval base in Newfoundland which had closed down a few months prior, and the building I had stumbled across was once the U.S. consulate established for the base, which was in the process of closing. I informed them of our family's immigration filing in Ottawa and asked them if they were in a position to assist us expedite it.

The employees were only too delighted to have 'something to do,' and within days they had transferred our files from Ottawa and after taking us through the formalities of finger-printing, handed us our green cards.

We were thrilled at our good fortune. All in all, it took just three weeks from the time I walked through their door to the time we had our immigration permit, a far cry from the twenty-four years in England, or even the three offered in Ottawa.

As I said, perspective is everything.

Upon returning to Montréal and with green card in hand, we had to figure out where in the United States we wanted to go. I wanted a place that offered a good standard of living and plenty of job opportunities. After extensive research, we decided on California, and selected San Francisco because of its European charm.

On a Saturday in mid July of 1969, the movers came and packed all our household goods into a truck and left for San Francisco. We had planned to start driving the next day, hoping to reach the West coast before the movers did. While having breakfast the next day, I saw an advertisement in the local paper by the Boston-based engineering firm of Stone & Webster. They were looking for civil engineers and conducting interviews that same day at a hotel in Montréal.

I talked it over with Eliza and decided I had nothing to lose by going to the interview to see what they had to say. So we delayed our departure to California by a few hours and I went to the interview.

As you may have already guessed by the inclusion of the story, I was hired on the spot. They even offered to pay all our expenses to make the move. Since I wasn't familiar with Boston, they offered to fly me there the next day and show me the city. After returning from Boston that evening, I told Elizabeth about the old world charm of the city and how it reminded me of England, and we made the decision to accept their offer and move to Boston.

On Saturday we had sent the movers off to San Francisco with our things, and on Tuesday we drove across the U.S. border at Champlain into Vermont on our way to Boston, starting another brand new chapter in our lives.

We checked into a hotel with our infant son on July 20, 1969, a date familiar to people all over the world as the day Neil Armstrong became the first man to walk on the moon. It was a surreal experience to enter the lobby of the hotel and watch Mr. Armstrong take his 'giant leap' for mankind. I couldn't help but think of the giant leap my family had just made

In the meantime people at Stone & Webster Engineering Co. had located the moving truck just outside of Chicago, had it turned around and redirected it to Boston.

After spending a few nights at the Hotel, we rented a two-bedroom apartment in Brookline on the edge of the medical district of Boston. One of our neighbors was a young doctor from New York doing his residency at a local hospital. We hit it off immediately and became close friends. He had a young wife and baby daughter, so we had a lot in common.

Every morning I took the subway to my office at Stone & Webster in downtown Boston, while Eliza would stay at home with Darvish. I know it was difficult for her at first, settling in to a new neighborhood not knowing anyone, so she would often take our son for long walks around the area in his stroller, trying to meet other young mothers and make friends.

It was an adjustment for both of us, even little Darvish. He was a colicky baby and cried a lot. One evening out of sheer frustration, we left him in his crib and let him cry his heart out. It was hard to do so, but one of the mothers Eliza had met on her daily walk had sworn by it. Two hours later the police knocked on our door to make sure everything was all right. Apparently a neighbor upstairs had called the police.

From then on we decided to try other methods.

My responsibility at work at that time was to help design and build a new fossil fuel power plant in Virginia. It was challenging work and I enjoyed it, but I still had the stock market in the back of my mind, calling me like a siren's song.

IV.
1970's

Boston, Massachusetts – U.S.A.

"Taking to the Street"

AFTER MOVING TO Boston, I transferred my meager brokerage account at Bache & Co. to their local branch, and every day at lunch time I would take a short walk over there from my office to check my stocks and chat with their brokers. I was a small timer to them, but they appreciated my enthusiasm and we had a good time.

They had a Ping-Pong table in their basement, which I soon took advantage of and beat them all. The brokers constantly challenged me, but none were able to even come close to beating me. I may have been an amateur investor to them, but they definitely respected my game. I used the table as an excuse to pick their brain. More and more I began to think my future was not what I once imagined it would be.

As time went by, I gradually became disillusioned with engineering and my prospects in the profession. I was very good at my job, but I was just too ambitious and energetic to be confined to a nine-to-five job in an office for a fixed salary with annual increases that barely kept up with inflation.

So after two years of working at Stone & Webster, I began to look at alternative careers. With a young family and a new house with a big mortgage, switching careers was a real risk. After all, I had gone to school and trained as a civil engineer; it was really the only job I ever had aside from transitory, part-time college jobs.

But I just wasn't happy. My first choice was to become a stockbroker since I had been totally captivated by my penny stock success. Failing that, as a backup I could pursue my childhood hobby and become a carpenter.

While I was pondering all this, I joined the local YMCA and played pick-up basketball every day after work. It not only kept me in shape, but it was also quite therapeutic after a full day at the office. Most of the players were blacks from a nearby housing project. One of them was called Lefty, a good player who couldn't afford the admission fee to play. He would get word to me on the basketball court and I would stop my game and go to the check-in desk to pay the five dollars for him so he could come in and play.

I got along very well with the basketball guys from the neighborhood. We came from very different backgrounds, both socially and economically, but basketball was our common language. Just like I used Ping-Pong to better commune with my stockbroker friends, basketball was what bound me to those young Black men from the projects.

Even today, I make a point of going to a fitness club for my daily exercise, and it all goes back to those days in Boston.

One of my colleagues at Stone & Webster was an Indian fellow who was married to a German woman. One evening they invited my wife and me to their house for dinner, and afterwards he announced that he had a surprise for us, something he knew we would find tremendously entertaining.

I looked at Eliza and shrugged as he went into the other room, having absolutely no idea what was in store. He came out with a tape recorder, which he set down on the coffee table. He left the room again. I smiled and nodded at his wife, who giggled and raised her eyebrows as if to say, '*Wait till you see this!*'

Now we were getting excited. I had no idea what was going to happen. Perhaps he had written a song ad was going to play it for us.

He came back out of the other room with a cassette tape, and put it in the machine, and paused a moment before hitting the start button with a flourish.

What came next I would never have guessed in a million years.

There was what seemed like several minutes of room tone, just the sound of the tape turning. Eliza and I politely waited, and then we heard it. It was a gentle murmur, followed by gurgling, and then a loud fart.

They had recorded the sounds of their six-month old son sleeping. It was their first child and they were captivated by the sounds of their baby.

Eliza and I just sat in stunned silence as the tiny snores, gurgles, and occasional farts of their child were proudly shared as if it was the most brilliant entertainment ever created.

Needless to say, it was an unforgettable evening, although not as they intended.

In June of 1971, I resigned from Stone & Webster and began applying with brokerage firms for a position as a stockbroker. Just before abandoning engineering altogether, as a personal challenge, I took the Pennsylvania Professional Engineering Examination. Passing that test was a coveted and prestigious title that meant the ultimate success in engineering. I passed with flying colors.

I would not have felt good leaving the profession unless I knew in my heart I would have succeeded.

The initial reaction to my interest in Wall Street was extremely discouraging. None of the brokerage houses had ever had a foreigner with a funny accent apply to enter their sheltered domain. E.F. Hutton even gave me a psychological test, the results of which said I would make an excellent engineer but a poor stockbroker.

But I was determined. And the negative reactions and obstacles only made me more determined. I continued to pursue positions at other brokerage firms until I finally made positive impression with two of them. One was a small regional firm, Wise, Voisen based in Worcester, which was about an hour's drive from Boston. The second one was the large national firm PaineWebber, with two branch offices in Boston alone.

Wise, Voisen had a lot of empty desks and were anxious to fill them up, so they offered me a position as a stockbroker trainee without any hesitation. But I was far more interested in PaineWebber since it had originally started in Boston in the late 19th century, and was a much larger firm with a great reputation. They had offices throughout the U.S., and furthermore, was still a partnership, which indicated to me that there would be lots of room for growth.

I filled out the employment application and took a written test similar to E.F. Hutton's, and every day I called the local manager to ask about my test results. His name was Lewis and I'm sure he was either tired or impressed by my persistence, and after about a week he called me in for an interview.

The meeting lasted about an hour, during which time he asked me a number of questions, trying to size me up. Lewis was in his late 30's and quite perceptive.

After the interview, I again kept calling him every day looking for results. About a week later he sent me to the larger branch office in downtown Boston to be interviewed by a senior partner, a typical New Englander with a degree from Harvard and a three-piece pinstripe. He had devil of a time trying to figure me out.

Finally, after two more weeks of waiting and calling, they offered me a position as a full-fledged stockbroker, with a modest salary and six months of training. The first five months were in the branch, and the final month would be in New York City in a classroom with 32 other trainees from all over the country.

When I filled out the employment application on the first day, the senior partner suggested I consider changing my name to something more conventional, like George Smith. I told him I would think about it and let him know. In the end I decided to keep my name, which turned out to be a great decision since people tended to remember "that broker with the funny name."

At the end, I took the necessary exams, secured my series 7 and NYSE license, and became a registered stockbroker. I was given a desk and a telephone and told to go to work and prove myself.

Like a hungry lion out of a cage, I unleash all my talent and energy toward that goal. I was building a business, which for most part was within my own control. My destiny was in my own hands, which was exactly what I wanted. Lewis would hold regular weekly sales meetings and give all 34 brokers in his office pep talks and direction. In a private session, Lewis told me that I had failed the psychological test, but a convincing argument in my favor was the response he'd received from my old bosses at Stone & Webster for reference. They were very happy that I was not going to a competing firm.

Obviously, he knew he had a tiger by the tail.

The majority of the brokers in the office were in their 30s, as was I, and worked quite hard. It was a very competitive atmosphere. My primary responsibility was to seek and obtain new clients and bring in their investable assets, thus building a good customer base. Even though the focus of the firm was cold calling, I was given the flexibility to explore other prospecting options.

After a few weeks of cold calling with mixed results, I began to send out mailers by the hundreds offering literature on tax-free municipal bonds. The term "tax-free municipal bonds" was a phrase everybody had probably heard before, but few people understood. But everybody understood "tax-free." So the mailers generated interest. Slowly but surely, responses started coming in as a result, which gave me a huge boost in morale and really got me excited about my prospects.

Typically, after receiving a response I would mail them the brochure promised in my letter, and a few days later I'd follow up with a telephone call offering my services. Most of the time I managed to get my foot in the door and would drive to their home or office regardless of the time of the day to present myself as being someone 'at their service.' It was not common for stockbrokers to go out of their way and drive, sometimes quite a long distance, to visit a prospective client. I found the receptions warm, and the longer the distance, the better the reception. I would canvas primarily the New England states like New Hampshire, Rhode Island, Massachusetts, and Maine.

After visiting a prospect for the first time and spending a few introductory moments with them, they would usually get comfortable and open up about their financial concerns. By listening and answering their questions and addressing their investment concerns thoughtfully, I would slowly but surely gain their trust and confidence.

On one occasion, after I had made initial contact with a Harvard University professor and sold him a $5000 tax-free bond over the phone, I arranged to visit him at his office the next day. As it happened, I had bicycled to work that day, and at the appointed time, I hopped on my bicycle and peddled over to Harvard Square in Cambridge.

I locked my bike and presented myself at his office. The man was in his late 60's and a typical absent-minded professor. I was not at all surprised that he taught philosophy. After a brief introduction, he informed me that he needed to sell some securities in order to pay for the bond he had just purchased from me the day before.

He then pulled out a black notebook from his desk drawer and handed it over to me. It had a list of all his holdings, but it was laid out in an inefficient and confusing way. This was a good opportunity for me. I told him that he could deposit all his securities in a single account at PaineWebber, where we would keep track of everything, collect his dividend, and clip his bond coupon and send it to him at the end of each month.

He liked that idea, so I pressed on.

"Where do you keep your certificates?" I asked.

"Across the street," he answered, and pointed out his window at a local branch bank. "Let's go take a look."

This was going very well. He was practically doing my job.

We walked across the street and I waited in the lobby while he went to his safe deposit box. After about fifteen minutes, he returned with two large brown shopping bags containing his securities. He handed them to me and I followed him out the door. This was a turning into a very good sales call!

I started to follow him to his office, but he stopped me on the sidewalk.

"Why don't you take those over to your office and deposit them for me?"

"Sure. Let's go up to your office and I'll write you a receipt," I said, surprised at how easy this was going.

"You can mail it to me," he said, shaking my hand and leaving me standing there on the street with two bags of securities.

Suddenly I realized I had a real dilemma. Namely, how to carry those two bags back to my office safely on my bicycle. I ended up calling my office manager from a payphone asking for help, since this was before cell phones. He sent one of the office personnel in a taxi to take the securities, and I had a very excited bike ride back to the office.

It took the office staff two full days to record all his positions and deposit them in his new account. I had been handed over two million dollars worth of securities, a million had been in bearer form, that is there were no names printed on the certificates

Basically, I had been carrying around a million dollars in cash in two brown shopping bags.

This story got widespread attention at my firm and became known as the 'bicycle story.' It was recounted at the training center as well as offices as a good example of how to acquire a worthy new client.

But the person who learned the most from it was me. After that, it occurred to me that maybe all the professors at Harvard were good prospects. I obtained a copy of their alumni list and sent my mailer to the lot of them, resulting in about a dozen new clients, one of whom was a law professor and advisor to President Reagan.

Another client, who was professor of physics at Harvard University, walked into my office one day to deposit a check he had just been awarded for winning the Nobel Prize for physics.

Another interesting experience from the early days of my career was my contact with a businessman in upstate New Hampshire. I drove about 140 miles to visit him at his factory, a steel fabricating plant. We initially just chatted while he asked me a bunch of questions trying to size me up and get comfortable. He told me that he crafted Stradivarius violins as a hobby, and that he owned two originals made by the maestro himself, each of which were worth in excess of a million-dollars. He told me that he played them in a local orchestra.

When we finally got around to finance and investments, he informed me that he owned a substantial quantity of tax-free municipal bonds. I convinced him to sell his bonds and reinvest the proceeds in a tax-deferred annuity, which was a new product in mid-70's, and he'd never heard of. After a bunch of questions, he signed the annuity application and handed me several hundred thousand dollars worth of bearer bonds.

I was on a high the entire two hours it took to drive back, and as soon as I walked in the door, the office manager told me that right after I had left the factory office of the businessman in New Hampshire, he called to verify my employment.

It had suddenly dawned on him that he could have handed a small fortune to a total stranger who may or may not have been who he said he was.

In general, I found dealing with small business owners far more productive and gratifying than most other professionals. They make decisions quickly and are loyal clients, as long as you're straightforward with them. They're used to dealing with vendors and others and appreciate a straight shooter who will go the extra mile.

Or 140 miles.

By 1973, my business began to take off and I began to enjoy the fruits of my labor. I moved my family to a larger house on four acres in a posh suburb of Boston called Chestnut Hill. The same year, just as I predicted when I applied for a job, PaineWebber took their stock public from a partnership via a complex transaction involving the purchase of a publicly traded mutual fund.

By custom, every year our office manager would invite select top producers to dinner at a fancy restaurant in Boston as a reward for their success. In 1973, I was included. Eight of us went to Locke-Ober, one of the oldest and most exclusive restaurants in Boston. Until a few years prior, they had even restricted women from all but one small dining room in the back of the restaurant. The building is listed in the national Register of Historic Places.

So it was with much ceremony and purpose that I walked into the private dining room with my peers. I had a great sense of accomplishment when I sat down at the beautifully crafted table with my co-workers. I remembered with satisfaction all the difficulty I had even getting an interview with a brokerage. I was the guy with the funny accent, so different from what was expected, and yet I had worked hard and succeeded. In Boston, no less!

In the phrase of many great movements, 'I had a seat at the table.'

When it came time to order wine, for some reason the sommelier handed the wine list to me. Not knowing much about wine at the time, I just selected the most expensive bottle of red wine on the list, which was a 1959 Chateau Lafite Rothschild, at $56.00 a bottle. Keep in mind this was 1973. A loaf of bread cost about a quarter and a gallon of gas was thirty-five cents.

Everyone loved my choice, and we ended up ordering bottle after bottle until our party had exhausted their entire inventory of twelve bottles of that particular vintage. The next morning I walked into the office with a sizable hangover, as did a few of my colleagues. My manager approached me carrying two things: In one hand he held one of the corks from the previous night's wine bottles, and in the other was the restaurant bill.

"Ahmad, the total cost of our meal last night was $210.00."

I just looked at him. It sounded reasonable to me, actually much less than I would have thought. I remained non-committal, waiting for him to continue. A good businessman always knows when to speak and when to keep quiet. Since I had no idea where he was going with this, I remained silent.

"The wine tab was over $700."

Oh. So that was where he was going.

He wanted to know why the amount the firm spent on liquor for a single meal was equivalent to the cost of a fairly decent used car.

We all laughed about that evening for years, but the following year they kept the wine list away from me.

I had a client who loved the action of the market, and would call me several times a day to enquire and make trades. He reminded me of me and my penny stocks.

On one occasion he sold short 1500 shares of Avon. When the stock rose and his losses mounted, he complained to our manager, claiming that he had not authorized that trade. He actually accused me of making the trade without his knowledge. This was a profitable client, and so the situation was treated very seriously. After a lengthy meeting with the senior partner of the firm, it was suggested that if I wanted to keep my job, they would cover his short and hold me personally responsible for any losses. They took his side of the story and would not compromise.

I was not happy about that decision, but I was very happy with my job, so I agreed and paid back a total of over $27,000 over a period of 12 months.

As my income increased, I began to develop an appreciation for the finer things of life. I had worked hard and felt like I deserved to live well. That was why I had immigrated, after all. To have a better life.

After moving into an even bigger house, my first major purchase along those lines was a used Rolls-Royce, which I bought sight unseen. The car had been advertised in the Wall Street Journal. I called the owner down in Florida and made the deal over the telephone. I was very excited about my purchase, and couldn't wait to get behind the wheel.

Now all I needed was someone I could trust to go down there and drive the car back to Boston.

There was a 17-year-old boy named Tommy who worked in the mailroom who also ran errands for us in the office. I thought he was trustworthy, and when I approached him with the idea his eyes lit up like it was New Year's Eve. He was almost *too* excited, I thought, but I needed a driver.

"I just need to ask my girlfriend," he said.

I thought that was funny, as he was only seventeen and he already understood married life.

The next day he said it was a go, and asked permission to take his girlfriend along for the ride. It would cost more because I was covering all the expenses, but I agreed. I could see he was almost overwhelmed with excitement at the idea of driving such a beautiful car across the country with his girlfriend at his side. I remembered how I felt when I bought my first little car, a Mini in 1961.

How incredible would it have been to drive a Rolls at that age!

Plus, I figured he would probably be even more careful with her in the car with him, since nothing would be so embarrassing to a young man to do something foolish in front of his girlfriend.

So he and his sixteen year-old girlfriend flew to Tampa the very next day, checked the car inside and out, and handed the owner my check. In accordance with my instructions, Tommy would call me periodically from a public phone and report his progress. He was always right on schedule. I was glad I had agreed to give them both this little adventure.

Three days later he arrived in Boston, and after washing and waxing the car, he delivered it to my house. Now it was his turn to watch the look ox excitement on my face. I was thrilled and delighted with my acquisition. Having lived in England for years and having witnessed the class distinctions over there, I felt like an English aristocrat.

I left the Rolls in my garage and went to the office the next day. When I returned at the end of the day, of course the first thing I did was rush to the garage to look at my prize.

All the windows in the garage doors had been painted over with dark blue paint.

I went inside and there it was, my Rolls-Royce, untouched and unharmed.

I asked my wife about the windows.

"I did that," she said.

"Why?"

"I didn't want any of my friends to see your car," she answered.

I understood immediately. A few years earlier, Eliza had begun writing plays, and in doing so, had become a part of the local literary scene. The circles in which her friends traveled were not those of a typical stockbroker's family. For the most part, they were penniless hippies, and we were denizens of the bourgeoisie.

She did not want to be embarrassed by the opulence of my car.

I did think it humorous that for anyone to look through the windows of the garage, they would first have to drive through a wealthy neighborhood and approach a very expensive home, but I let that slide.

As I've said, a good businessman knows when to speak and when to remain silent.

A year later I bought my first Ferrari, a used 1967 chocolate brown 330 GTC with a 12 cylinder engine. This time I picked it up myself. When I drove the car from Springfield to Boston, I was immediately struck by the noise. It was a very loud car to drive after the Rolls, but it certainly had a lot of power, which was why I bought it in the first place.

In the years to come, as I became more established, I kept adding to my car collection. I eventually had to build a second garage to accommodate them. Among my favorites were a '73 Ferrari 365 GTB Daytona Coupe, a '72 Ferrari Dino Spider, a 1952 French Citroen, two 1965 Mini Cooper S's, and a 1961 Morris Minor.

I enjoyed taking them out on the road, depending on my mood. It was almost like choosing an outfit.

I now understood why women have so many different pairs of shoes.

———————

My younger brother Ali moved to Boston to attend MIT, and had become politically involved with a radical group of Iranian socialists who would hold anti-Iranian government meetings from time to time and discuss what should be done about the Shah's corrupt government. On one such occasion, Ali borrowed my Rolls-Royce and drove it to the meeting. When he returned, he told me everyone at the meeting had loved the car so much that they had decided, after the present government in Iran was overthrown and their regime took over, they would make sure that everyone drove a Rolls-Royce.

Now that's my kind of socialist.

———————

Since I was doing a lot of driving visiting prospects and clients, I asked my firm for a monthly expense account. This was actually unprecedented at PaineWebber, but I brought in quite a lot of business, so after some deliberation they agreed to grant me a $300 monthly allowance.

This was just another example of my growing stature within the company, and it felt good that I could blaze a trail for such a perquisite.

———————

One of our colleagues at the office told us a story that I doubt any of us ever forgot. It was so outrageous it almost sounds like a joke, but he swore it was true.

His elderly mother had recently gone skiing for the first time. Apparently there was a company with a booming business taking busloads of old ladies from the Boston area to the slopes of Killington Mountain in New Hampshire for day skiing. They would pick them up and have them back at the end of the day, renting them the equipment and including basic instruction to get started.

Once they arrived, they would be outfitted, given a quick lesson, and then taken to the chair lift to the novice slope.

Soon after this, my colleague's mother had the urge to urinate, and the guide, not wanting to take her back down and leave the others, suggested she go behind a bush to take care of her business.

As soon as she dropped her ski pants and squatted behind a tree, her skis began to move, and before you know it, she was flying down the slope out of control, shrieking all the way. The other old ladies saw her pass by, bare-assed and screaming, and so they began to follow suit. Screaming, I mean. They did not, as far as he knew, drop their pants on the way. The guide charged down the hill after her and finally brought her to a stop near the bottom of the hill.

At the end of the day, they all gathered at the lodge for a drink before departing for Boston. A tall, attractive older gentleman with his arm in a cast entered the bar and sat down near them.

Now, a handsome older man sitting near a group of older women, many of whom were probably widowed, naturally attracted their attention, so one of the women asked him about his arm to engage his conversation.

"Are you a beginner, dear?" she asked sweetly.

"No, actually I've been skiing since I was a child," he answered.

"Oh, my. Whatever happened?"

"I was skiing down the hill, minding my own business, when I heard a scream and turned to see a woman racing down the beginner slope with no pants on. I got so distracted I hit a tree."

None of the ladies could bring themselves to explain to him the reason for the distraction, but one in particular seemed especially red-faced as they bid their goodbyes and went out to their bus.

I don't know if that's really what happened, but it sure made for a good story.

It was around this time that the first electronic calculator was introduced to market by Bowmar Instruments, a Massachusetts-based company. This tiny machine that could fit in your pocket caused a sensation, and their stock advanced considerably until competitors started to come out with more sophisticated and cheaper versions. Some performed quite complicated mathematical functions for the time.

Meanwhile, after just three years as a stockbroker, I had reached the top position in my office. By 1975, I was number one in the entire firm out of over a thousand brokers. My production grew year-by-year due to my relentless pursuit of new clients, and I reached the magic one million dollar level of production in 1979, the first individual in the history of PaineWebber to reach that threshold.

In appreciation, my manager gave me a statue of a businessman holding a briefcase. It was inscribed with the words, "Million-Dollar Man."

More than anything else, that milestone meant the world to me. I had achieved something that no one in the history of the company had ever accomplished, and I had done it my way.

It was a long way from Isfahan to Wall Street, and I had arrived in style.

As my business grew, so did the number of assistants I needed to help me deal with my ever-expanding client list. By 1980, I required two full time secretaries and a registered broker just to answer the phones and assist me with the conduct of my daily business.

In 1975, I became a U.S. citizen. My heart was with my homeland, but my life was here. My office threw a party on my behalf with a citizenship cake and champagne. It was a beautiful gesture on their part. It felt great to be appreciated that way, and was the perfect end to a momentous day.

My Citizenship Cake with my manager

That same year, I took my family on a vacation to California. We flew from Boston to Los Angeles and stayed at the Beverly Hills Hotel. We had planned to stay in Los Angeles for a few days and then drive up the coast to San Francisco. However, the morning after our arrival in Los Angeles, I received a call from my office manager informing me that the Fresno office had heard of my presence on the west coast and had made a special request that I talk to their brokers about the secret to my success.

So instead of driving up the scenic coast, we took the eastern route through the desert up to Fresno. I was flattered, and enjoyed sharing my methods to the other brokers, and afterwards the manager of the office wined and dined us and put us up in the best hotel in Fresno.

It wasn't the Beverly Hills Hotel, but it's the thought that counts.

A couple of years later I took my family to Hawaii for a week's vacation, and of course a similar request was made by the Honolulu office. I felt like the rock star of PaineWebber. I was to make my presentation at the end of their workday, which was 10:00 in the morning because that was when the stock market closed in Hawaii, so I would have the entire day afterwards for whatever I wanted to do.

I would not be surfing.

When I walked in, I was surprised to see a roomful of guys in shorts and flowered shirts, just like a typical tourist. When I asked about it, the manager laughed and said that they were in full compliance with the local dress code.

My industry was pretty formal, with suits and ties the expected norm, and this fit well with the nature of the business, which is competitive. So it was pretty interesting to tell a bunch of guys in Hawaiian shirts how to aggressively attack their business.

Over the years I received many requests to travel and visit PaineWebber offices in different parts of the country and share the secrets to my success. The feedback I received was very gratifying, and I was told my motivational speaking had a definite impact. I was glad to help, but from my own experience, I knew my encouragement would help some of the brokers more than others.

You can lead a horse to water, as they say, but you can't make him drink.

Unless the broker was willing to put in the hard work, they were unlikely to follow in my footsteps.

Occasionally a broker would call to consult me regarding a specific situation he or she was facing, and ask for guidance and directions. To those brokers I gave my full attention and respect. That is the type of thing I had done when I was investing in penny stocks. I picked the brains of those with more experience. By helping others, I was making an impact on the industry.

I think it is an inherent quality within all of us to leave a legacy. We do this by having children, who carry our blood-line into future generations. We can also do this by affecting change in the world around us, whether it be physical or intellectual.

By assisting other brokers within my industry, I was making a mark, the same as I would have made as a civil engineer who built a road or a bridge.

In mid 1975, I met a stunning Irish girl with long blonde hair. We began an affair, which eventually became so intense that I moved out of my house, bought a condo close to my office, and began to live the life of Reilly. We would take off most weekends and fly to a nice resort in Bermuda or the Bahamas and just party and live it up.

My father had a saying that described what was happening: "When a man grows wealthy, his house becomes too small and his wife turns ugly."

In America, they just call it a mid-life crisis.

Whatever you call it, I was having a good time.

But when the honeymoon was over, we got down to the brass tacks and realized that we were from two different walks of life. Neither of us could imagine a long-term relationship, and after a year of fun in the sun, my wife and I started to see a marriage counselor. Within a few months I sold the condo, said goodbye to the blonde, and moved back to my house with my wife and son.

But of course, nothing is ever that easy.

Soon after I broke the news to the blonde, she got drunk, went to my condo, and absolutely trashed the place.

I can't say that I blamed her.

A few months earlier, while I was still living in the condo, my wife had taken the Ferrari for a drive, and upon returning home had rammed the car into the snowplow blade I kept in the garage to clear our long driveway during the winter months.

Sheer anger and the 12 cylinders don't mix, and vengeance was hers that day. The entire front of the car was smashed. Hell hath no fury like a woman scorned with your car keys.

I suppose I had that coming, too.

I had become quite close to one of the brokers in my office. Irv was single and had in a condominium not too far from the office. It was a true bachelor pad, with a fire pole, a coffin, and a parrot that squawked out the foulest language imaginable non-stop.

I don't know if Irv had the place because he was single or whether he was single because he had the place, but no wife would have put up with that glorious excuse for a home in a million years.

Irv wasn't the only guy who used the place as a bachelor pad, either.

It wasn't just for bachelors, of course.

A number of his favored friends, including a few high-powered politicians, were provided keys to his kingdom and booked his place for a night or a few hours at a time. It reminded me of the film "The Apartment" with Jack Lemmon.

Irv was quite a character. He used to send out specially made, provocative Christmas cards every year. They became so popular he used to get requests from senators and congressmen to be put on his mailing list.

After several years, Irv's Christmas cards had become so popular that he had to stop because of the cost.

Pretty impressive for a Jewish bachelor.

One day I went into another brokerage office to visit a friend and saw the most beautiful woman I had ever seen. This stunning brunette was the receptionist. I did not approach her directly, but instead asked my friend if he could ask her discreetly if she would like to go out with me sometime.

Much to my surprise she agreed, and so one evening I took her out to dinner, and afterwards took her to Irv's condo.

Irv's Christmas cards

I had not given him prior warning, but the night was going really well, one thing led to another, and I couldn't pass up the opportunity.

Fortunately, the place was empty. I don't know what I would have done if there was someone else there, but that wasn't the case so I wasn't going to waste time thinking about it when I had something much more enticing to engage my attention.

There was a bottle of champagne on ice, so we helped ourselves and had a wonderful time. The next day when I went to the office I made a point of thanking Irv for his thoughtfulness and hospitality.

He gave me a blank look.

"What are you talking about?"

"The champagne. At the condo. That's a nice touch."

His eyes grew wide and for a moment he looked stunned, but then he broke into a wide smile and started to laugh. When he finally stopped, he explained that the one of his high-powered politician friends had booked the condo for that night, and my lady friend and I had polished off his special libation for the evening.

Now it was my turn to laugh. I hoped the mayor wasn't basing his seduction only on inebriation.

In the spring of 1975, Irv invited me and my wife to join four other couples for a week on a small island in the Caribbean. This was my first break since joining PaineWebber in 1971. Part of the British Virgin Islands, Marina Cay turned out to be a quaint little place accessible only by boat. There were just eight wooden huts, with a tiny bar and restaurant. The island was managed by Irv's best friend.

We were the only occupants on the island, and spent our days snorkeling, laying on the beach, and exploring nearby islands. The bar on the island used an honor system, whereby you just helped yourself to any drinks and wrote it down in a ledger. Whenever you left, you tallied it up and settled the tab.

At breakfast one morning, a member of our group offered me what he called 'Window Pane.'

"What's that?" I asked.

"It's a vitamin."

I looked at him skeptically.

"Trust me, you'll like it," Jimmy said with a smile.

Famous last words. He handed me a small tab of brown paper and told me to swallow it.

I took his word and went about my day, eventually forgetting about it until a couple of hours later when we boarded a small boat to visit another island.

Suddenly, my head started to rise above my body, and I began to see and feel my surroundings from a totally different perspective. The looked down and the water seemed to be solid, like a sheet of ice. I laughed joyously. How could there be ice in the Caribbean? The ice turned to glass, and then back to water, except the water was now a vibrant pink.

I looked up at the sky, but now it was water and for a moment I thought I was upside down. The colors, scents and smells were constantly changing, and magnified in their effects. Everything I sensed was intensified, and everything was beautiful.

A jet plane buzzed right past my ear, but it turned out to be only a fly, which shook hands with me and politely flew away.

"So pleased to make your acquaintance," buzzed the fly, and disappeared into the mouth of a smiling shark, which disappeared just as quickly.

But my euphoric state had a downside. For the next twenty-four hours I was so high I couldn't eat or sleep, and I felt so hot I had to continually jump in the ocean to cool myself off.

I decided LSD would go the way of surfing, at least as far as I was concerned.

Back in Boston, I attended an evening art class at the local high school and learned a lot about artists and their history. Up until then, I knew very little about art. It reminded me of my modeling days as a teenager, and I found the course very refreshing. At the same school the following year, I took courses in making Pizza and Calzone but never got around to practicing them in real life.

I was a little restless during this time, but it was a good restless. It was borne of happiness, not turmoil. I was almost like a kid again, drinking in every aspect of life, exploring and investigating and having a good time. I had always been a curious person, and I was indulging myself in whatever struck my fancy.

Every year while my son was growing up, I would take him trick-or-treating in our neighborhood on Halloween. Like all children, he loved getting dressed up as a pirate or a hobo and getting his bag filled with candy, and I enjoyed watching him.

In 1977 it was so cold that I decided to drive him door to door in my white Rolls-Royce. I would drive up to each house and Long John Silver would pop up and ask for his treat. The reaction of some people after watching the little pirate take his treats back to the large white Rolls was priceless.

That was the most fun Halloween I ever had.

In the mid-seventies, my office formed a softball team called the Boston Blue Chips. Since baseball had not been part of my culture, and I had been only exposed to it after I moved to the U.S., they proclaimed me the owner and inscribed number 8 ,7-8. on the back of my shirt. In those days stock prices were quoted in fractions of eighths, so it was an amusing joke.

We would compete once a week against other brokerage teams, and I would basically act as a cheerleader-in-chief for our team.

In July of 1979, one of our colleagues on the team who was well connected arranged for us to have a softball match against President Carter's White House staff. We all flew down on a Friday with our families and spent a pleasant weekend in Washington, DC, and came home with gifts and souvenirs embossed with the White House seal.

We also beat the President's team 9-7.

One evening I asked my friend Jimmy, the one who had given me the LSD, if he wanted to go out to dinner. He gladly accepted and when I showed up in my white Rolls to pick him up, he had two beautiful black girls with him, and the four of us had a great meal at a fancy restaurant. Afterwards, the police pulled me over with some excuse about a turn signal and asked a bunch of questions.

I think their real suspicion was seeing the two Black beauties in the back seat with Jimmy, who was also Black, in the front passenger seat. After they were gone, Jimmy lit a joint and told me that two girls in the back were transvestites.

Jimmy was full of surprises.

Upon Irv's initiation, a group of five couples arranged to go to the Caribbean for another week's vacation in 1977. This time however, he had chartered a large boat so we could cruise from island to island.

When we arrived at the Boston airport, there seemed to be five men and six women, but in the typical confusion of a group leaving n a trip, no one asked any questions. By the time we arrived in BVI and boarded the boat, it became apparent that Irv had invited two of his girlfriends without telling them about the other. One was cute and petite, the other big and buxom. I'm sure he was salivating at the thought of getting those two in the sack together, and for a little while I thought he was going to pull it off.

The first night on the boat everything seemed harmonious, but the next morning I heard a shriek, and turned just in time to see girlfriends number two, the big, strong Italian beauty, actually picked Irv up off the deck and pitch him into the sea.

Irv then had to climb out of the water and clam her down long enough to take her to shore, where he arranged for her to fly back to Boston.

Irv had a lot of guts.

On our last day we rented a catamaran owned and operated by an elderly couple who had retired from the States. They took us for a nice day's outing on the ocean, and toward the end of the day and after many drinks, the old man began to blow a horn.

Badly.

If that wasn't painful enough, his wife then stood up and began to sing, also badly. Even though we were all a little drunk, it was pretty annoying.

I almost wished girlfriend #2 was back. She could have thrown them over the side.

In 1977 I was featured as PaineWebber's number one broker in an article published in The Registered Representative featured on the next two pages, our industry's leading trade publication.

Over the years that followed and as my name became more and more widely known, I was interviewed many more times for many publications, including Eastern Airline's inflight magazine.

Have you discovered the most effective means of communicating with your clients? Ahmad Fakhr has, and it has helped make him Paine Webber's top retail broker for the second consecutive year.

Ahmad selected individual, personalized contact as the most successful method of communicating with his clients, the key ingredient which led him to his present level of production in just a few short years.

The unusual twist to this success story, however, is that Ahmad Fakhr (pronounced "far") was probably one of the least likely candidates to succeed in the brokerage business when he set his sights on becoming a registered representative in 1970. He had been in the United States only two years and had virtually no contacts from which to build a client base. A native Iranian educated in England, he had worked as a civil engineer in Canada, so he was certainly not a "home-town boy."

But when Ahmad came to work for Stone & Webster Engineering Corporation in Boston, his fascination with the ins and outs (ups and downs, too!) of the stock market led him to spend many of his lunch hours at his broker's office, listening and watching and learning. His account was a small one, but he says, "I was just buying and selling and enjoying it." It was during these noontime visits that he began to notice the sharp contrast in personalities between the engineer and the broker. ("The engineer-atmosphere was too boring for me," says Ahmad. "I was working hard, but with no sense of accomplishment.") Thus, Ahmad set his goal: to become a broker, indeed, the best!

Undaunted by his lack of sales experience, he began knocking on brokerage house doors in Boston. The reception was something less than enthusiastic. "No one wanted to hire a guy with a funny accent and no sales experience," he recalls with a grin. "Remember, very few firms were doing any hiring at all in the early Seventies."

One of Ahmad's strongest characteristics, however, is perseverance. After several visits from this determined engineer, "Paine Webber called my bluff," as Ahmad puts it, "and gave me a desk and a telephone, saying,

'Show us.'"

For the next two or three months, Ahmad spent all his time cold calling, trying to establish a client base. His first efforts did not produce noteworthy results. "People just did not open up to a telephone call from a stranger," he admits.

Step two was the direct mail approach. He purchased mailing lists and began sending out standard Paine Webber mailers. "My wife and I addressed envelopes day and night," remembers Ahmad. "The response to these mailings averaged about 6%, and I telephoned each and every person who responded," he explains.

Those phone calls, though, did not follow the format one might expect from a broker-prospect conversation. "My goal at that point was not to solicit business," he explains, "but to arrange to meet with this person. I wanted to get to know them. And I wanted them to get to know me, and to begin building confidence in my ability to provide them with a service."

Once Ahmad began meeting potential clients in person, he began opening new accounts at an impressive rate. "The combination of direct mail, telephone and personal visits was the right one for me," he proclaims. "But my work really started with that personal visit. I used the time to determine a potential client's goals, his concerns and his financial requirements. Then I returned to the office to draw up an investment 'game plan' tailored to meet that client's specific needs." Ahmad is quick to emphasize that these "game plans" cannot be prepackaged, because people's investment objectives differ.

"A second in-person meeting included a written presentation of my ideas and suggestions. This was the meeting where I was looking for orders, and more often than not," he

says, "I left that session with a new client." However, all of this was very time consuming and the accounts he opened were relatively small. "I had to find a way to reach the big guys," said Ahmad. He thought about what people with money all have in common: — taxes. So he zeroed in on tax-free bonds, and geared his pitch toward judges, pilots and other business professionals. The accounts Ahmad acquired in this audience were significantly larger, and as always, he was careful to give them his special, personalized attention.

When one converses with Ahmad, the word "service" keeps popping up. While he is convinced that personal contact produces more new clients and generates more business than any other approach, he is just as convinced that those clients must receive outstanding service if they are to remain active on a long-term basis.

The attention Ahmad devotes to his accounts is above and beyond that required by Paine Webber. "You notice my phone doesn't ring incessantly the way some brokers' phones do. This is because my clients have no reason to call," he explains. "They know what we're doing." In addition to phone calls and personal visits, he provides each and every client with a comprehensive monthly tabulation on what the account is doing, and a year-end tabulation of all the account's transactions. These data are updated in Ahmad's office daily so that if a client should call with a question, the answer is readily available. Ahmad believes this is very important.

Today he still follows the same formula when opening a new account, whether a referral or one he has prospected himself. "When I get on the phone, the first thing I ask is 'when can we get together? Let's have lunch,' and so forth." Most of Ahmad's new accounts average $75,000-$100,000. While he won't turn down a referral account of less than $25,000, he says he doesn't actively seek them out.

What makes Ahmad's clients trust him so much? "You have to sell yourself," he says, "and the best way to do that is in person. You're not selling a product, but rather your knowledge and professional service." (There's that word 'service' again.)

The intricate servicing Ahmad has

AHMAD FAKHR
PAINE WEBBER'S NO. 1
by Janine Dusossoit

established for each account requires long hours of labor and much paperwork. "But it is essential, and after all," says Ahmad matter-of-factly, "it is merely a question of manpower." And *that* he does have: a full-time secretary and a full-time registered rep working exclusively for him. Paine Webber is investigating the possibility of a computer terminal for Ahmad's office linked to Paine Webber in New York to handle the phenomenal amount of processing which accompanies his accounts.

Ahmad finds the reception for prospects much better outside of the city —

the suburbs, New Hampshire and Maine are where more than 50% of his clients live and work. He goes out on business calls two days a week. On the average, he opens 15 new accounts per month, many of which are referrals.

On research, Ahmad is adamant. "Most brokerage house research isn't that good, and as for analysts, they know how to read the figures, but I

don't think most of them have a good feel for the market," he says. Ahmad doesn't rely on Paine Webber research, preferring instead to do his own, which he uses in conjunction with institutional research. He spends his Sundays reading, picking companies he thinks will prove good investments. Among his criteria are increased sales each year, increased profits, and what he calls the "technical action of the stock." He'll follow a company and when he feels comfortable with it, he might recommend it. Ahmad attends one analyst/broker luncheon per month.

Rarely will he recommend an OTC stock. "Big corporations need no introduction, so they seem to provide the safest vehicle." He pays a great deal of attention to new offerings and attends all office product seminars, but won't specialize, since he believes each client's needs are different. He looks for stocks for his clients rather than trying to sell the client on a cer-

tain stock.

These days, Ahmad is not working the 16-hour day, seven-day week he once did, although he still puts in long hours. To help himself relax, he takes four or five vacations each year, and enjoys basketball, tennis, ping pong and tournament backgammon. He holds a brown belt in judo. Ahmad hopes the new computer terminal at Paine Webber will free up more of his time, not for additional leisure, but for additional prospecting to expand his client base even further.

A new registered representative at Paine Webber who works with Ahmad has been following in his footsteps, utilizing the same basic techniques of personal contact and meticulous servicing. "His production," reports Ahmad, "has moved up steadily."

In looking ahead at the market and its performance over the next 12 to 24 months, Ahmad thinks it will "probably stay flat, the same as it has been for the past eight to nine months."

"I don't agree with those who believe the market will top the 1200 mark," says Fakhr. Regarding the market's future, he says, "It's hard to predict. A lot will depend on President Carter and what he does."

No matter what the market does this year, Ahmad Fakhr will open approximately 180 new accounts, probably gross between $600,000 and $700,000 and continue exuding the dynamic vitality and magnetic charm that symbolize his success.

Of himself, five years from now, "Who can tell?" Ahmad laughs. "If you had asked me that five years ago, what could I have said?" ●

I was also invited by the Advisory Council of Boston University to join as a member for providing advice and consultation on financial planning.

The August 1982 issue of the Boston Globe featured an article written about me entitled "An engineer turned successful broker".

A reprint from
BOSTON GLOBE
8/10/82

In the News

An engineer turned successful broker

INVESTOR'S NOTEBOOK

By Brendan Boyd
Universal Press

Boston's Ahmad Fakhr came to America in 1969 as a civil engineer. But he soon grew frustrated with engineering and quit to become a stock broker. He had to start from scratch, calling prospects cold and making appointments to meet them at home. By 1976, Fakhr was Paine Webber's top-grossing broker. This model career switcher credits hard work and shrewd investment decisions for his rise. His current stock picks: Colgate-Palmolive. Boeing, Con-Ed, AMF (high dividend payers), Standard of Indiana, Exxon, Getty (oil asset plays), G.M., Westinghouse (turnarounds). Data Switch, Data IO (emerging growth companies), Western Union, Warner (telecommunications).

When stocks rally, depressed issues rise fastest. When the economy rebounds, fundamental industries recover first. Those are two good reasons to get back to basic stocks, says Sanford C. Bernstein's president, Lewis Sanders. Sanders believes the economy is "about to recover – strongly," and that many cyclicals are irrationally depressed, particularly: autos (G.M. and Ford could earn $7-$10 in 1983), housing (Ryan), cement (Lone Star, Kaiser), forest products (Georgia Pacific and Champion International, both selling at twice Bernstein's 1986 projected earnings), steel (Inland, "a high-quality, low-cost producer"), aluminum (Alcoa, Alcan, Kaiser), and chemicals (Union Carbide).

With social security reform still floundering, American investors are turning increasingly to private retirement plans. Boston's **United Business Service** believes CODAs (Cash or Deferred Arrangements) may soon eclipse IRAs as America's favorite tax-deferred retirement vehicle. CODAs are employer-sponsored pension plans. Employees contribute a portion of their pre-tax salaries. These contributions accumulate and earn interest until retirement. Withdrawals cannot be made before age 59½ unless the participant is disabled, dies, retires or changes employers. Withdrawals are taxed as ordinary income. Deferrals of 15 percent are possible with CODAs. There is no penalty for hardship-induced withdrawals. And employees can have both IRAs and CODAs.

Investor's Notebook is a digest of opinions from financial advisers. No endorsement is implied or should be inferred. For further information, firms cited should be contacted.

I was also invited to present seminars on financial planning and investinments aboard Queen Elizabeth 2 on a cruise from Miami to Southampton, England.

Ahmad Fakhr presents a
Paine Webber Financial Seminar
and Investment Workshop

In 1978, I was invited to be a member of a panel of four scheduled to speak to several hundred brokers at a seminar held at the Waldorf Astoria in New York City. Admission was $300 a head, and the huge room was standing room only. The sponsors later marketed and sold an audio recording of that event for $28 each.

Nowadays the tickets would be $1500 and the seminar downloaded to iTunes.

Around that time, I started to look into leaving PaineWebber and starting my own brokerage house. I was doing very well, but even for me, 60% of all commissions was retained by the house. When I brought this up, the divisional manager called me into a private meeting at his office and countered by proposing to set up my own division within PaineWebber.

That arrangement would enable me to split the office profit with PaineWebber 50-50, in addition to my commissions. I was also free to recruit brokers from outside the firm, even encouraged to, thus leveraging the bottom line. And my startup costs were nil.

The idea appealed to me, and as a result, the "Fakhr Financial Planning Unit" was set up later that year, and I added four more brokers, all recruited from other firms. I had the best of both worlds, and my income almost doubled overnight.

It is ironic that the same brokerage houses that were rejecting me just a few years ago were now dangling millions and clamoring to recruit me.

I was so overwhelmed with my growing business that I decided to hire a personal assistant. Irv referred a young man named Chris as a candidate, and I hired him on the spot. Chris had a charming disposition and was extremely sharp for a twenty-five year-old. I made him responsible for paying all my bills, taking care of my automobiles, and even household errands.

At his suggestion and to minimize the cost of insurance and registration, I set up a corporation named Far Car, and reregistered my automobiles in its name. I also set up a bank account for the corporation to keep track of my automobile expenses. I did not, however, give Chris any signatory power. He wrote out all my checks which I would sign before sending out.

Once in a while Chris would report that he had used the Rolls-Royce as a limousine in his off hours and hand me a few hundred dollars that he had charged. I saw no harm in that, but didn't encourage him since I obviously didn't need the income. Overall I was pleased with his services, but in early 1982 when the Commonwealth of Massachusetts started to question the purpose and the legitimacy of Far Car, I asked Chris to dissolve and terminate the cooperation and close its bank account.

In 1979 PaineWebber acquired the research firm of Mitchell Hutchins, which was run by a bright guy named Don Marron. A year later, Marron became CEO of PaineWebber and began expanding the firm. In 1980, we bought the medium size brokerage house of Blyth, Eastman, Dillan, adding several hundred stockbrokers overnight to PaineWebber's already expanding numbers.

Blyth, Eastman, Dillan had had a policy of rewarding their large producers by taking the top 1% on an annual all-expenses paid trip to an exotic locale. After the merger, their brokers wanted the tradition continued and demanded the same of PaineWebber, and that year for the first time, they took the top 1%, which included me, plus spouses, to a beautiful resort in Santa Domingo for five days.

There were 26 brokers who qualified that first year. The annual tradition continued throughout my career, and we were taken to some of the most desirable exotic places in the world. Paris, Rome, London, and Monte Carlo were just a few. We stayed at five star hotels and were showered with gifts every night by the firm.

That was a good merger.

In 1979, as Iran was engulfed in a bloody revolution, I applied to the state department and secured immigration visas for my older brother Reza, his wife Houri, and their 13 year-old daughter. They came to Boston, bought a house, and Reza established himself as an import-export professional in textiles, which was his area of expertise.

Unfortunately, the revolutionary regime came down hard on my father because he owned a piece of land which he had inherited from his father. As a result, he donated it to the city and they converted it to a soccer stadium, which was named after him.

That same year, my good friend Toni and I signed up at the Skip Barber Racing School and took a three-day defensive driving course at the Lime Rock track in Connecticut. The automobiles were Crosby Formula 3 racing cars. They taught us the best way to stop, steer and take corners. It was another dream experience of a boy that I experienced as a man.

Later that year, I spent three days at Orvis Shooting School in Vermont to learn to use a shotgun. My wife's foster brother Peiter, who was visiting us at the time from England, accompanied me. The first evening after school, the two of us went to a classy restaurant located next to a beautiful stream and a table with a view overlooking the entire valley.

When our waiter first appeared, I pulled out a $100 bill and ripped it in half. I gave him one of the two halves and told him that if he did a good job for us, he would get the other half at the end of the meal.

Needless to say, the service was excellent.

Overall, I'd say the '70's were just as good to me.

V.
1980's

Boston, Massachusetts – U.S.A.
"Building an Empire or Fame,
Fortune, and Fraud"

IN EARLY 80'S I started conducting a series of seminars on financial planning. This was not only informative to the attendees, but a great way to attract potential clients, which was, of course, my primary motivation.

Every few months I would conduct a presentation in a different location, traveling all over New England. My seminars would bring in as many as three hundred people at a time, and those lectures turned out to be one of my most successful strategies for finding new clients. Over the years I added several hundred new clients to my already large base, and expanded my list to over four thousand at its peak. It was a very innovative strategy that was copied by others who came after me and even institutionalized to a degree. But it wasn't for everyone. It was a lot of time and effort.

The reason it was so important to constantly find new clients is because attrition is inevitable. The nature of the brokerage industry is such that any broker, no matter how sharp, will tend to lose clients over time. Some die, some lose money, some just transfer elsewhere. If someone moves, they have a tendency to take their money with them.

I'll never forget one evening in 1981 when a Jewish friend and the son of a wealthy client of mine, a newlywed, invited my wife and me to his apartment in Boston for dinner. It was a wonderful dinner. We were served lobster, exquisite wine; everything was exceptional. At the end of the evening as we were to depart, he told me that our share of the dinner was $125. I was too shocked to do anything but reach for mu wallet and pay him in utter disbelief. He came from an extremely well-to-do family, and yet he'd treated our evening as if it was some fraternity beer bust. We rushed out of there as quickly as possible, not knowing whether to laugh or cry.

In early 80's, my sister Shahla, who was living in Iran at the time, decided to send her thirteen year-old daughter Cathy to the States to live with us. Since she was about the same age as our son, we welcomed the idea. Both my wife and I felt she could be a good companion to him. Iran at that time had been torn apart by the revolution, and ravaged by the invasion of Saddam Hussein and his Iraqi forces. It was a war that lasted ten terrible years, and left nothing but destruction and hundreds of thousands dead on both sides.

Ayatollah Khomeini had dismantled the Shah's defensive forces soon after taking power, and so decided to recruit all the teenage boys in Iran and send them to the front like cannon fodder. Not having any arms to give them, and with no training, he gave them a copy of Koran as their only weapon and wished them well. Over 100,000 young boys perished with nothing but a copy of Koran in their hands.

Soon after Cathy's arrival, my wife decided to hire a cook to help prepare dinner once a week. She found an eloquent French lady who took a real delight in shopping and preparing the most exquisite 4 to 5 course meals followed by desert and coffee every Thursday evening.

I have to laugh when I think back to my son and our niece, neither of whom had an appreciation of such things, instead choosing to eat simpler foods, such as cream cheese on toast.

To each their own, I suppose.

In 1980, my old friend and colleague Irv mentioned that an old warehouse in Newport, Rhode Island was being converted to condominiums and suggested we take a look at the project. The building, which turned out to be an old fish market, was right on the water in the marina, and Irv and I each bought a one-bedroom unit on the second floor overlooking the harbor.

When we went to Newport Furniture to buy furnishings for the place, the owner, a 68 year-old Jewish fellow, told us a fascinating story. Apparently, he had come down with an illness a couple of years earlier, and a local doctor who had initially examined him for chest pains diagnosed him with terminal cancer. The doctor predicted he would live no more than six months. Having heard this, he left his wife of forty years and moved in with his young secretary in a high-rise condo on the waterfront. He had even abandoned his anti-German beliefs and treated himself to a brand-new yellow Mercedes convertible, something he would have never done before.

He told us that when a year went by and nothing had happened to him, he visited Massachusetts General Hospital in Boston, where after extensive testing, he was diagnosed with a mild case of bronchitis and was sent home.

He enjoyed his new lifestyle so much that he never wanted to go back to his wife. Some might have reacted differently, on either side of the diagnosis, but he chose to believe that he'd found quite a silver lining in a very dark cloud, and never looked back. As I said, to each his own.

Newport was an hour and a half drive from Boston, and on occasions I would drive down and use the condo on weekends, but it was primarily used by friends and selective clients who wanted to get away and shack up with a girl for a night or two.

I had learned from Irv the benefits of such ready accommodations.

Every time I cleaned up the place, I would find odd objects like a woman's shoe, or underwear, and other such things. I sold the condo a few of years later just to de-clutter my life.

Maybe that lesson came from Jack Lemmon.

In July of 1982 at Irv's suggestion, I signed up for an eight-day white-water rafting trip down on the Colorado River through the Grand Canyon. I was accompanied by my 13 year-old son, my older brother Reza, Irv and his girlfriend, plus one of Irv's friends with his girlfriend. The seven of us flew to Denver, where we were picked up by the outfitter and driven to a motel about an hour away. We were told that we would get picked up the next morning and driven to the river where the rafts were waiting for us. We were also told that each passenger was allowed a six-pack of beer and no more because of the limited weight.

Irv, being mischievous by nature, went to the local liquor store and came back with a trolley stacked high with boxes containing all kinds of alcohol.

When the outfitters saw this the next morning, they had a fit. They could not believe their eyes at Irv's total disregard for their instructions. They protested vigorously, but Irv would hear none of it. He insisted that he would not go on the raft without every last drop of his booze.

Nevertheless, they took us along with a few other passengers and all of Irv's liquor in a school bus to the river where two large rubber rafts were waiting. Each raft carried eight passengers plus a crew of two young river boys. They distributed the liquor between the two rafts and placed all the cans in burlap bags and tied them to the raft submerging them in the water for buoyancy, and also to keep them cool.

The trip turned out to be a delightful and rewarding experience. Every night we would set up camp on the hot sandy banks of the river while the crew prepared dinner for us. They would also dig a hole somewhere behind a large boulder to be used as an outhouse. The water temperature was a cool 48 F, just perfect for the beer but quite chilly for bathing. At the end of each day, we would all jump in the river, jump back out, soap ourselves up, and then jump back in for a quick rinse. It was quite energizing, actually, and relaxing around the fire with a cold beer after that always made it taste spectacular.

During our eight days on the river, we went over 48 rapids, some as high as 12 feet tall. It was thrilling, but also pretty hair-raising. The crew had trained us to tie a rope around our waist and hold on tight to avoid being thrown off. Throughout the journey, the outfitters would point to objects on the shore like small boats, or even plates and spoons and other personal effects that had been left there by those pioneers who never made it out of the canyon alive.

Whether that was true or not, I don't know, but given the rough waters I could easily believe it was, and their point was well taken.

During our entire time on the river, we had no contact or communication with the outside world whatsoever. We were over a mile deep in the canyon and unable to receive even radio reception. This is before cell phones and laptop computers, of course.

July 4th fell on the fourth day of our trip, and that evening Irv set up a makeshift bar and served cocktails to everyone while one of the crew played his guitar. Ice for the cocktails came from a few large blocks that they carried to preserve the food.

Sitting around the fire, drinking cocktails on July 4th in the Grand Canyon, was an experience none of us would likely ever forget, and it was then that everybody appreciated Irv's foresight.

I watched Irv behind the 'bar' mixing drinks and graciously receiving thank-yous, even from the crew who had thought he was crazy, and thought to myself, *this is a man in his element.*

Irv was put on this earth for such things, and we were all the better for it.

After eight days and just before reaching Lake Mead, our trip came to an end and we all disembarked, tired and happy. Some walked up the canyon while others elected to ride mules

Celebrating July 4th on the river

to get to the top, where a small airplane waited to fly us to Las Vegas.

As soon as I checked into Caesar's Palace, I called my office to check in. Eight days was a very long time to be incommunicado in my business. I was informed that my banker called several times about an urgent matter.

When I contacted the bank, they informed me that the Far Car account was overdrawn to the tune of $50,000. This came as a total shock since I had instructed my private secretary Chris to close that account several months earlier. They also told me that there had been a lot of activity involving large sums of money in all of my bank accounts recently. I smelt a rat from a distance.

I flew to Boston the next day and arranged for Chris to meet me at my house that same evening. He showed up with his older brother Gary and confessed to having abused my bank accounts by forging my signature and kiting checks among three different banks.

I listened incredulously as Chris confessed he had stolen over $70,000 and bought seven automobiles and started a limousine service on the side, all while I was rafting through the canyon, blissfully unaware of his shenanigans.

Chris had become jealous of my success and wanted to try and replicate it. I made him deliver title to all seven automobiles to the bank the next day and then fired him on the spot. Apparently he had used the corporation bank account as a conduit to move money around and run his limo business.

The bank sold all the limos and came after me with a lawsuit for the $40,000 shortfall. We set up a meeting, and with my attorney's help we reached a settlement that resulted in me paying $20,000 to the bank to get them off my back.

That turned out to be a very expensive river rafting trip, indeed.

A few months after his dismissal, I received a call from the FBI requesting information on Chris. Three agents came to my office and questioned me for over an hour. They were very polite, and when I enquired as to the nature of their involvement, they informed me that Chris had taken it upon himself to present himself as a PaineWebber financial advisor. He had printed business cards and contacted elderly, retired people and promised them a high rate of return on any money they invested with him. Obviously his charming disposition, which was one of the reasons I had hired him in the first place, had opened other doors for him, as well.

Through his fraudulent Ponzi scheme, Chris had managed to swindle investors out of 1.5 million dollars. He had bought a $700.000 house in Weston, an affluent suburb of Boston, and a $25,000 diamond ring for his girlfriend whom he had presented to the investors as his wife. They had him arrested and he was waiting for trial.

In the meantime, his girlfriend had gone back to the same investors, telling them that $100,000 bail money was needed to get Chris out of jail! She promised them the return of all their invested money as soon as he was released. Unbelievably, some of them threw good money after bad and she apparently was able to collect the $100,000, but she flew to Brazil and disappeared.

In 1983, a group of us consisting of my brother Reza, my 14 year-old son Darvish, his close friend Brian, and good old

Irv and his girlfriend embarked on a five day hike in the mountains of New Hampshire. We followed designated trails during the day and stayed in huts each night, all of which we had booked months in advance.

During breakfast on the second day, Irv announced that he and his girlfriend found the hike a little strenuous and would instead drive to Montreal, Canada to spend a few days there.

I carried a flask of Bacardi 151 rum with me, which Darvish and Brian took swigs from on occasion to 'refuel,' as they called it. We enjoyed the balance of our hike, and when we descended I called my office, who informed me that the stock market had just exploded on the upside on heavy volume.

The media attributed this to Reagan's policies, which led to lower inflation and lower taxes. The bull market of the 80's, with the exception of a major but short-lived drop in 1987, would continue well into the 90's.

That trip more than made up for the trip down the river, I have to say.

In 1980, Reza's brothers-in-law, the "H" brothers who were living in Austin, Texas, suggested I buy a piece of land there for investment purposes. They located a seven hundred-plus acre parcel in Georgetown, just north of Austin that they felt was attractively priced.

I flew down over the weekend and ended up buying it at $1,200 an acre with two other partners, my brother Reza and a friend of his who lived in Toronto. During our initial inspection as we drove around the property, we saw groups of whitetail deer running around. I bought a rifle, and every fall I would fly down to Austin, hook up with the H brothers and we would all go deer hunting and have a grand time.

After five years, our partner in Canada ran into financial problems and needed capital, so we agreed to sell the property. I conveyed our decision to the brothers in Austin and asked their help in finding a potential buyer. Sure enough, after a short time they came up with a buyer and we sold the land for $2000 an acre, making a decent profit.

Unbeknown to me, the two brothers had gotten together with a wealthy Texan and talked her into going into a partnership with them, whereby the elderly woman would put up all the capital for buying the property, and the brothers would offer their 'expertise' in its development in exchange for a 50/50 split of all subsequent profits. Needless to say, that was very sweet deal for them. Anytime you can get someone else to take on 100% of the risk and reap 50% of the profits, that's quite a deal!

I gradually found out about their arrangement and also discovered that the price we received was a fraction of the fair market value at the time of the sale. I had just been too buried with my own business to question the offered price, and never spent the time researching and checking the market price in that area. In fact, shortly after the sale, my neighbor, a rancher whom I had never met, sent me a handwritten note saying that he would never have accepted such a price even in a fire sale.

I was upset, of course. I had trusted them to steer us in the right direction and come up with the highest possible offer, but the brothers instead had drummed up this scheme to swindle me and my partners out of hundreds of thousands of dollars just to enrich themselves behind our backs.

They sold that same piece of land a year later for $4000 an acre, twice what we had received. I'll have more about this melodrama starting on page 135.

During one of my hunting trips to Texas in the early 80's, back when things were good between us and before all the swindling, the H brothers approached me to join them as a third partner to form a company to buy land and build single family houses in Austin. They needed my financial backing as well as my good credit. Under my personal guarantee, a local bank agreed to provide the necessary financing.

Since I was heavily involved in running my own business in Boston, I left all the management and administration to them. As you might guess, that was another mistake I made because I trusted them.

The first two houses they built were sold successfully and made a good profit, or so they said, but they had run out of money trying to complete the next two houses. Again with my personal guarantee, the bank provided the necessary capital to complete the project. I found out later that the older brother had siphoned money out of the corporation for his personal use.

They ended up taking possession of the houses themselves for their own personal use, but they were unable to carry the huge mortgage for very long and I was forced to pay off the bank notes personally. Eventually, both houses were sold and I recovered most of my out of pocket capital.

Shortly after selling the land in Georgetown, I started to look on my own for another piece of land in Texas. After looking at a few parcels one weekend, I bought a 1000-acre ranch about 100 miles west of San Antonio. The owner was the CEO of a major oil service corporation, and was extremely helpful in advising me and putting me in touch with the right people to manage my ranch.

I had an eight foot fence built around the new property and stocked it with exotic animals like Axis and Fallow deer, Blackbuck antelopes, Red Stags, Zebras, Aoudad Sheep, and several other species of wild game. I drilled three water wells and built lakes next to them. Water was pumped into the lakes using windmills. I built a log cabin on one of the lakes and would fly down several times a year, rent a car at San Antonio airport and spend a few days at the ranch relaxing and hunting, mostly with friends and family.

It should be noted that, while whitetail deer management and hunting is regulated by the state and has a specific season, exotics can be hunted all year-round without a permit. Many Texas ranchers stock their property with exotic games and invite hunters all year round to come and shoot them at a price. Some even carry super exotics like Zebras and Giraffes. Prices vary depending on the game and can run into many thousands of dollars.

Every time I left the hustle and bustle of the big city and my busy life and drove through the gates of my ranch, I felt like I had arrived at my own personal oasis. It was almost like a magical place to me. It was so peaceful there that if you hadn't just come from the airport you'd never imagine there was another world out there. At night, the sky was painted with an ocean of endless stars.

I hired a local cowboy, named John Tom to keep an eye on the place, visiting and checking things out once every few days. He was a typical Texan, the strong, silent type. He did his job and never asked too many questions, and didn't offer much conversation unless engaged, either.

Once I asked him if he had traveled much.

"I went down to South Texas once," he replied.

He had never been outside a 150 mile radius from the ranch, so to him, Texas was the entire world. He would often bring an old friend to keep him company, a man named Charlie who was well past 80. Charlie was the opposite of Tom, very open and talkative. Before I had the water wells drilled, I asked them how I could determine the best location for drilling, and Charlie showed me how the Indians found groundwater: He cut a small tree branch with a fork like a wishbone and started walking around the ranch pointing his 'divining rod' toward the ground.

When the points of the fork merged together like magnets, it indicated underground water. Sure enough, the three locations picked by Charlie using that method all hit water just over 130 feet below the surface.

Another time John Tom called my office in Boston to tell me my four Red Stags had somehow escaped to a neighboring ranch despite the high fence around my property. I made a few calls to other ranchers to pick their brains, and was told of a professional helicopter service that would drop a net over the animals, hoist them up, and set them down inside my fence.

That was something I had to see.

I hired such a service and flew down that weekend to witness the operation. After spending over $2000 and many hours, the operation was a total failure, and I returned to Boston empty-handed. A few days later I received a call from John informing me that the Red Stags were back on my property. He explained that Charlie had opened the gate and simply sprinkled a bag of corn around on the ground. After many hours of patiently waiting, the Red Stags slowly worked their way back to my ranch eating the corn and Charlie just closed the gate behind them.

Talk about simple solutions!

After he passed away a few years later and I hired a replacement, a friend of John named Earl who told me that John would bring his sons and other family members without permission to hunt on my ranch and do whatever they liked in my absence.

Maybe that's why he wasn't too talkative.

A few years later I had a 14,000 gallon tank built to store water for our use on the ranch. When I decided to have it painted, I asked my son if he or any of his college friends at the art school would be interested in covering the round tank with murals. He had just received his BA from Tufts University in Boston.

Two girls, one Russian called Ania and one American, named Michael accepted the challenge and drove down in a beat-up VW to my ranch in Texas. They worked for three months and created a mural reflecting life and the game on the ranch. They even painted in my ranch manager with his trusty revolver by his side, watching over things.

Later on, after the girls had returned to Boston, I heard that the cowboys were trying to figure out what the girls were supposed to be doing, and had come to the conclusion that they were "for Mr. Fakhr's pleasure." The gossip-loving locals just could not relate to murals being painted on the water tank by two outsiders, I guess.

There was a convenience store at the junction of highway 41 & 83, just four miles before reaching my ranch. It was called Garven Store and run by a Texan and his wife. The

My ranch and the water tank

store was the nearest civilization for 50 miles, and I enjoyed stopping there on my way to the ranch to chat with the owner. Over time I got to know them fairly well. They were simple, country folk, much like some of the villagers I had grown up with.

I've traveled all over the world, and if you take away culture and language, people are more alike than different.

On one such trip from Boston, I brought them two live lobsters as a present. By the time I flew to San Antonio, rented a car, and arrived at their store, it was close to midnight. I had to wake up the husband to deliver the lobsters, and so only gave him brief instructions on how to cook them.

On the way back four days later, I stopped by and asked them what they had thought of the lobsters.

"Well sir, they were pretty tasty. But I'll tell you, those shells were a little tough."

I had to stifle a laugh. Apparently, not knowing any different, they had tried to eat the whole thing, shell and all. The next time trip, I brought them two more live lobsters, this time with complete instructions. Now knowing how to cook and eat them, they found a world of difference and really enjoyed them.

They were nice people, but tough. I wouldn't doubt they had eaten the first two lobsters, shells and all, just to be polite.

In 1980, PaineWebber had a new president who was a hunter, and we became quite friendly. He invited me to a bird hunt in 1983 at an exclusive club in upstate New York, about a three-hour drive from Boston.

There were six in the group, and typically we would be positioned around a field and they would release birds like ducks and pheasants from a central tower and we would shoot anything that flew our way. We also got up early every day and hunkered down in blinds waiting for geese to fly over, but were not having much luck.

While walking back to the club for lunch, I spotted a solo Canadian Goose walking along the lake. I got my shotgun ready and crawled through the grass on my hands and knees shot him dead, only to find out that I had shot the club's pet goose. I was quite embarrassed and offered to pay for it, but they wouldn't accept it.

After a couple of days of hunting in the club, while driving my Audi Quatro back to Boston from the club, I ran into an 18-wheeler that was crossing the Potonic State Parkway. My car was totally destroyed and I was taken to a local hospital in Rhinebeck, New York. I had a broken left arm, three broken ribs, and a concussion.

I nearly died, and was out for three days, partially due to the fact they had injected me with so much morphine. Reza and my wife Elizabeth drove down from Boston, and she stayed with me until she could arrange for an ambulance to carry me back to Boston.

At Massachusetts General Hospital, a metal plate was screwed onto my broken arm. While recovering at home, I kept in touch with my office and clients, and with the help of my three associates, kept the business going. Ironically, PaineWebber paid me $25,000 a month disability income while I was recuperating.

In 1984, the same hunting buddy and president of PaineWebber called me to New York for a personal meeting. He informed me that the compensation arrangement granted to me six years earlier was too generous and would have to be modified. After extensive discussion and bargaining, it was decided that I would abandon the FFPU (Fakhr Financial Planning Unit) and forego sharing the division profit in exchange for increasing my payout to 50% from the normal 40%.

This resulted in a significant reduction in my income, but as I had been aware all along that the previous arrangement had been a unique and generous arrangement, I was not too concerned. I had probably been making more money than the president himself, facing me at that meeting. Besides, I had gotten disenchanted with managing a bunch of brokers under me and was more interested in focusing on the growth of my own business and servicing my clients.

It's worth noting that to the best of my knowledge, no other broker in the entire firm ever had such a lucrative compensation arrangement, before or since.

It certainly was good while it lasted.

My wife's playwriting involved putting productions together and paying actors and actresses to perform in her plays. One such actress, who also happened to be quite friendly with her, was an overweight woman who always seemed to be on a diet, something which never prevented her from downing a quart of ice cream for dessert.

One of my wife's plays was staged outdoors by Charles River, who had the heavy actress hunker down and threw a blanket over her. During the performance she was used as a large boulder for another actor to sit on. The night I attended, as soon as the actor sat down the rock farted really loud, and the entire audience burst out laughing. Since that night, I have referred to her as the "farting rock".

In the summer of 1983, my 14 year-old son and his best friend Brian talked me into going skydiving. We signed up and drove to New Hampshire and spent the entire morning in class being taught that art of jumping and all of the safety steps involved. After lunch, the three of us boarded a small plane with an instructor and when we climbed to 3000 feet, the copilot gently pushed us out of the plane. The parachute was on a static line, which meant we didn't have to worry about pulling a ripcord, the chute opened almost immediately.

I floated toward the earth in what I remember as almost total silence. It was exhilarating. By the time I reached the designated landing field, I had gotten the hang of the steering, and could have immediately gone back up for another try. I'm proud to say I landed on my feet and stayed on my feet, which is not how everyone does, apparently. Where the river rafting was rough and exciting, this was peaceful and exciting.

Neither experience should be missed.

Brian was a smart boy with up-to-date knowledge of everything related to computers, and the local police had hired him to run their computer system. This led to a rather amusing habit of my son's.

Darvish would drive his car to school every day, and park it illegally on the street right in front of the high school. Each day he would drive home with a parking ticket, which Brain would delete from the police computers. This lasted for over two years until Brian left his position at the police headquarters.

My son Darvish had another friend named Vikram, who came from a very gruff Indian father and a very hippie-like American mother. This boy was a real devil and always looked for mischief, but got along well with my son. One time when the two of them were on a flight together, Vikram walked the plane and cut off the bottom of all the sickness bags with a pair of scissors.

I suppose then he sat down and prayed for turbulence.

One morning my wife received an urgent call from a security guard at Bloomingdale's, summoning her to the manager's office where Darvish and Vikram had been detained. Apparently, the night before, Vikram had talked Darvish into hiding under a bed and spending the night in the store, helping themselves to the pastries in the bakery and who knows what other mischief after everyone had left.

Early the next morning, security saw that motion detectors had gone off during the night and released a security dog, who sniffed them out.

To teach them a lesson, my wife let them stew in the manager's office for several hours before going to rescue them, but rescue them she did.

Neither of them is welcome in Bloomingdale's to this day.

In 1986, my wife's cousin Simon moved from Australia to Boston and initially stayed with us. One evening I took him out for a night in town. We went to a popular restaurant and disco, and had a great meal. Afterwards, as we were standing by the railing overlooking the dance floor, two pretty girls approached us and asked us if we wanted to dance. We danced for a while and then had a few rounds of drinks.

By one in the morning we were half drunk, but the girls wanted to go to Chinatown for a late meal. After some good food and even more drinks, the girls suggested we spend the night at a nearby Holiday Inn.

On the way, I drove my Jaguar over some nails and got two flat tires. That should have been a warning to me, but as I said, I was half drunk and feeling good, so we abandoned the car and took a cab to the motel.

The girls picked up some coffee while I booked two rooms, and then Simon and I each took a girl and headed upstairs. The next thing I remember was waking up at noon with all my money and valuables gone. The girls apparently drugged our coffee. We took a cab to my house and passed out for sixteen hours.

A few days later I read in the local paper that a group of professional girls did this regularly, mostly to businessmen. One such individual claimed that the girl who had drugged him in a similar fashion had walked away with a suitcase full of cash totaling over $400,000.

Simon had quite an introduction to life in America.

In 1986 my sister Shahla and her husband also immigrated to the States and settled in Los Angeles.

I did not take my brother-in-law out clubbing.

In 1986, I met a Texan who specialized in custom-made cowboy boots, and I ordered four pairs of eel skin boots, which is a very soft, expensive skin. He made them in different colors and to this day I still enjoy wearing them. Shortly after he made the boots for me, the use of eel skin was banned.

Good timing for me. And the eels, I guess.

In the fall of 1987, the H brothers and I and another hunting partner flew up to Canada for a goose hunt on James Bay in Northern Ontario. After landing in Toronto, we connected to a flight to Timmins. From there we boarded a small plane operated by Austin Airways Ltd. and owned by the local Eskimos of Attawapiskat Village, our final destination. The village had a total population of 900.

When we arrived at the village airport, we were taken in pick-up trucks to the water's edge and transported by canoes to the campsite. Our accommodation was a wooden hut with four bunk beds, heated by a wood stove. Every day we we'd leave early in the morning and be canoed to a shore where our local guide would lay out a few decoys and start calling the geese without the aid of any instruments.

It was quite interesting to watch him open his mouth and then hear the sound of a goose come out.

Once, when a few ducks flew by, he immediately switched to duck calls and brought some of them in for us. He seemed like a simple, happy fellow, content with himself and his life's 'calling.'

During 1987, my wife's foster brother Peiter traveled from England to stay for a few weeks with us in Boston. Pretty quickly after his arrival, he got involved with the woman who lived next door. She had lost her husband a couple of years earlier to cancer, an apparently Peiter was just what she needed. He ended up moving in with her and staying for several months, but finally had to drag himself away from her and return to England. Shortly after, she mailed him a one-way ticket and begged him to come back to no avail.

In the late 80's, my son Darvish started taking a serious interest in Motocross, and for the next three years I acted as his crew chief, coach, and mechanic. Almost every weekend during the spring and summer I would pack his bikes in a trailer hitched to the back of our SUV and drive to another motocross event in New England. I would train him and coach him to drive as hard as he could.

Not only was this a great bonding experience as father and son, his motocross racing became a nice diversion from the long hours and weekday grind of the office. Even better, he started winning all of his races and collected a bunch of trophies, which was quite impressive to all of his high school friends. Later in life, he told me that all my pushing taught him how to be competitive and strive for higher goals.

One night Darvish, while at high school was invited to a party at the house of one of his friends. He borrowed my colorful Versace shirt for the occasion, and when I saw him the next day and asked him how the party had gone, he told me all the girls had gravitated to him. He was the hit of the party. I felt such pride until he told me he couldn't tell if it was him or the shirt that attracted them. We had a laugh over that.

He entered college and spent his first year at Bradford in Massachusetts, sharing a dorm room with a classmate named Nick from New York City. Naturally, his mother and I missed him a great deal, although I was also excited for my son to be out in the world. I remembered how I had felt when I left home for London all those years ago, and knew I would enjoy hearing about his experiences at school.

In high school, Darvish had a white cat that he had named Cocaine, and unbeknownst to us, he took his pet with him to the dorm at Bradford. One evening he called from college and told his mother that school officials had discovered Cocaine in his room and confiscated it. My wife nearly had a heart attack, with thoughts of our son's expulsion from school and a criminal record racing through her head, until Darvish laughed and explained to her that he was talking about the cat.

During his second year he transferred to University of Colorado in Boulder and while there, he shared a house with four other boys from school. Once in a while I would ship him a large box with nuts, chocolates and other goodies, which the five of them would immediately devour. They couldn't wait for the next one to arrive.

One night his roommates sent him out to buy some beer because Darvish had a fake license and none of them were old enough to purchase alcohol. When the liquor store owner asked for his ID, he presented the fake one. The man, still suspicious, asked Darvish for his zodiac sign. Darvish didn't know what to say because it was someone else's ID with Darvish's picture on it. Darvish got nervous and ran out of the store, the owner chasing him. The police were driving by and stopped him, but let him go with a stern warning. Apparently this kind of thing happens a lot in college towns. With thousands of students of all ages, it's a regular occurrence.

During his sophomore year, he discovered art for the first time, which greatly pleased his mother. He changed his major and ended up transferring to Tufts University in Boston to complete his degree. I was ambivalent at first. A man will always feel proud when his son follows in his footsteps, and I admit I thought perhaps Darvish would do so. But he loved painting and had a real talent for it, which pleased us both. In the end, all I wanted was for my son to be happy and to find his own way in the world.

After obtaining his BA from Tufts, he attended the Slade School of Fine Art in London, a world-renowned institution where he obtained his masters degree in art. He stayed in England, and as his work progressed he started to make a name for himself. He received a number of awards, including the prestigious BP Travel Award, and was commissioned for several portraits, one of which is permanently hanging at the National Portrait Gallery at Trafalgar Square in London. It's a portrait in nine panels of the famous dancer Akram Khan, and is quite stunning.

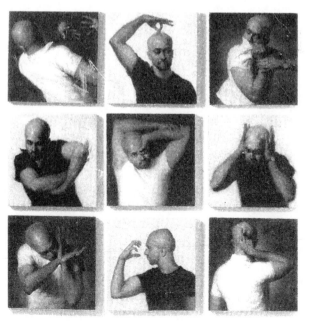

Akram Khan's portraits

Since my house sat on over four acres of land, we started using the backyard as a soccer field, and every Sunday, weather permitting, we would invite friends and family over for a friendly game. The word spread quickly, and eventually the weekly event became so popular that we had to turn people away. I also had a swimming pool built, and after each game we would all take a refreshing dip and then gather around the pool for food and conversation. I always enjoyed playing the host at these get-togethers.

One of the players who would come regularly with his wife and 8 year-old son was Dr. Bakki. The boy wore knee braces and mostly just run around in circles without being too effective. One time Simon kicked the ball high up in the air and Dr. Bakki's son, who was running around in circles as usual, lost sight of the ball and it hit him right smack on top of his head. He dropped like a stone, although he wasn't seriously hurt. It was obviously unintentional, but Dr. Bakki got very angry and accused Simon of doing it deliberately.

Dr. Bakki had always told everyone that he was a medical doctor and had worked in several hospitals in Boston, and of course everyone believed him including his wife. There was no reason not to. But a few years later, his wife found out that it was all a big lie. He was just leaving the house every day and spending his time doing who knows what and living off her money which she had inherited from her parents. It was such an embarrassing situation that the entire family moved to Los Angeles and no one ever heard from him again.

In another soccer game, one of the husbands tried to scissor kick the ball over his head, but kicked the ball right in his own face so hard that he passed out. It really was quite funny, and everyone was laughing, but when he didn't get up right away his wife began to cry and asked for someone to call an ambulance to take him to the hospital. Just then he came around, and everyone went back to playing the game, including him.

He didn't try any more scissor kicks, however.

During the 70's and 80's, the brokerage industry had introduced many new investment products in the form of partnerships. These included oil and gas, real estate, airplane leasing, and even movie production. Because of the tax structure and high tax brackets, the maximum at the time was 70%, these products had special appeal to investors. However, the partnerships carried very high fees and made a lot of money for the general partners and the industry, but sometimes very little for the investors.

As tax brackets dropped as a result of tax law changes, the appeal of these products diminished considerably.

Things were going great all through the 80's until October 19, 1987, known as Black Monday. Stock markets all over the world crashed, beginning in Hong Kong and falling like dominos as each exchange opened. Almost every investor, including my clients, lost a lot of money that day.

On that day the Dow lost over 500 points to 1738, a 22% drop and by the end of the month the U.S. stock market had lost close to a quarter of its total value.

Naturally, this caused real havoc all over the world, and I, like the rest of the industry, lost clients as a result. However, for those who stuck it out, it only took a few months for the market to start coming back. The market launched an unprecedented climb that lasted 13 years and took the Dow from around 1,200 to over 14,000. The age of Internet and dot coms had arrived.

After the crash of 1987, a large number of unhappy investors started filing lawsuits for "product failure" in those partnerships. Most brokerage houses ended up settling with investors but the details were almost never disclosed. The clients just wanted as much of their money back as possible, and the brokerage houses just wanted to go back to work as quickly and as quietly as possible in order to focus on making back their losses.

My neighbor, the one so taken with Peiter, was also a client of mine, and ended up suing me over the money she lost. Even though she was a close friend of my wife, she claimed her foster father, a powerful Jewish businessman, had persuaded her to file suit.

The 1989 'Chairman Council' trip of PaineWebber was originally planned for Vienna, but was changed at the last minute to Vancouver because of a hostage situation during the meeting of the OPEC ministers there. Since my wife was getting tired of these annual trips and refused to attend, I asked a hunting buddy who lived in Temple, Texas to join me instead, and he gladly accepted.

During every one of these annual trips, one morning was set aside for a 'sales meeting' for the brokers, primarily to satisfy the IRS and justify the expenses. The wives in the meantime, were taken on excursions and entertained elsewhere.

On this occasion, the wives were taken to a fur factory and showroom to check the coats. Some of them expressed an interest in looking at men's coats to buy as a present for their millionaire husbands. Since my friend was not in the business, he went along with all the wives and was asked to model the coats. When they returned, he seemed very excited, and explained the fun he had had trying all these different coats on and parading around in front of about forty women. I think I would have found that rather pleasurable, myself.

A few years later when we had our annual meeting in Paris, again my wife declined to go, and so I took her foster brother, Peiter instead. The first day we were given a bus tour of the city. Peiter started to flirt with our pretty Parisian tour guide. She was a tough one, but after three days he managed to wear her down and she agreed to go out to dinner with him on our last night there. He ended up spending the night at her place, and the next morning he arrived exhausted and just in the nick of time to catch the flight back to the States.

The next such trip was in London, and this time my wife accompanied me. The first night the firm had leased the prestigious food store Fortnum and Mason exclusively for the event, and they served us dinner, followed by a live band and dancing. Before leaving, everyone was allowed to take any item in the store as a gift. We chose a smoked pheasant and some exotic teas.

It was a special and meaningful night for me. Back in 1959, when I first arrived in London, I had walked by this same store and looked at the items in the display window with envy. They were all priced far beyond my meager student budget. There was a large Indian doorman dressed like a Maharaja, and he gave me such an icy glare that I took off in a hurry. It was obvious that he took one look at me and decided I did not belong in his establishment. From that day on, every time I walked down that street I made sure to cross to the other side when I approached the store.

To receive expensive goods as a gift because of my earnings for the company was a beautiful thing.

The only thing that would have made it better was if the doorman was still there.

VI.
1990's

San Antonio, Texas – U.S.A.
"Every Ending is a Beginning"

IN 1991, MY hunting buddy and PaineWebber president invited me to join him and a few others for a dove hunt down in Argentina. A group of six of us from all over the United States met up in Miami, where we kicked off our trip with a great dinner at the world famous Joe's Stone Crab restaurant. If you're ever in South Beach, I highly recommend it.

Stone crabs, (menippe mercenaria) are caught just a few months out of the year. They possess two claws of different sizes, the larger of which is the "crusher claw," and the only part used for consumption. If broken in the right place, the wound quickly heals itself and re-grows back over the next 12 months. Stone crabs are served cold, but to prevent the meat from sticking to the shell, the claws are cooked immediately before being chilled.

After dinner we headed for the airport and flew to Buenos Aires. We arrived the next morning and were picked up by a minivan and driven to a smaller regional airport and another flight to Bahia Blanca, a city about 700 miles south of the capital. From there we were driven to a chalet two hours away, where we relaxed for the rest of the day.

The next day we were off to shoot dove in the surrounding areas. It was a fantastic shoot. There were so many birds that every day we each went through several thousand rounds of shells and ended up downing over a thousand birds each. All the birds were piled up in the back of a pickup truck and taken somewhere locally where they were cleaned up and distributed among the local residents for consumption.

After 3 days of "volume shooting," we were all exhausted. Our shooting shoulders were black and blue from firing hundreds of shots each day, as you might imagine, despite using a special recoil pad to mitigate the effects. Even so, the thrill of our success was exhilarating.

When we arrived at the airport for our return flight to Buenos Aires, there was a serious sand storm and as a result the arriving plane had been delayed. One of the participants was a high powered businessman who owned two Lear jets was starting to make plans to have one of them fly from Arizona and pick us all up to save time. Fortunately our commercial plane landed after two hours of delay and we were able to make our connection in Buenos Aires and get back home on time.

I repeated this experience with this group of hunting buddies several more times for dove and pigeon hunts in Argentina over the next several years. It was not only great fun, but good for business.

During the trips I became acquainted with a couple of big shots from New York City who eventually became my clients, and enjoyed a good business and personal relationship with them up until my retirement.

In 1992, I received a notice from the Commonwealth of Massachusetts suspending my driver's license for a year due to three moving violations, primarily for speeding. My problem was that I always owned beautiful sports cars, and loved to open them up on the highways. How could I be expected to sit atop a thoroughbred and merely trot around the track?

There were times when I was able to talk my way out of a ticket, but for the most part the Massachusetts State Troopers were not sympathetic to my need for speed.

The suspension of my license presented a serious dilemma since I depended on my automobile not just for commuting to and from the office, but also for visiting clients and prospects.

I purchased an eighteen-speed mountain bike and appealed my case to the State, requesting a hearing to try and reduce my sentence. I happened to mention this to my good friend and ex-colleague Tom while we were duck hunting on his property down on Cape Code one day, and he jokingly said he would talk to the governor and see what he could do. Even though Tom's family was politically well connected, I thought nothing of it.

A couple of weeks later, my wife drove me to court for the hearing, and when I reported to the clerk, he looked up my case and informed me that my license had been reinstated and I could even drive home! I was so relieved that I went and bought a bottle of champagne and presented it to Tom and thanked him for helping me.

It pays to have friends in high places, or at least to go hunting with those who do.

In 1994 during a routine checkup, my doctor he informed me that my prostate-specific antigen (PSA) level had become alarmingly high. He referred me to a young urologist, who after many different tests including a biopsy, reported that he had detected cancer in my prostate and recommended that I have it removed.

Before taking any such drastic action, I decided to do some research of my own, something I think anyone should do in such a situation. As a successful broker, I learned to analyze the risks and rewards of multiple actions on which my own money and that of my clients depended, the least I could do was the same due diligence when it came to my health. It always amazes me that some people will count every penny and yet fail to be as careful with their health, including doctors themselves.

After reading up on the subject and learning about different options available, I consulted a well-known and established urologist for a second opinion. He put me through similar tests and informed me that my cancer was not that serious and I did not have to have my prostate removed. Instead he recommended monitoring it closely and checking my PSA every six months. To be on the safe side, I consulted with a third urologist, who confirmed that opinion.

I was extremely relieved, and so far I have monitored my PSA regularly and have had no reason to do anything different.

To think I might have simply taken the advice of the first doctor and had my prostate removed!

In business as in life, always practice due diligence.

Since PaineWebber had a corporate relationship with Carolco, a movie production company based in Los Angeles, in 1996 they invited a select few brokers from all over the country to join Sylvester Stallone for dinner in New York City one evening. The occasion was to arrange to raise capital for Carolco, which planned to continue making Rambo movies. I enjoyed chatting with him, but it was quite surprising to see how short he was in real life compared to the Herculean image he portrayed in his movies. I would estimate he was no taller than five foot seven.

His biceps, however, were quite impressive.

A few years later when the Chairman Council annual trip was held in Rome, our influential chairman Mr. Marron arranged for a private session with Pope John Paul at the Vatican. Regardless of your religion or beliefs, it is a truly impressive experience to meet the Pope.

As much as you imagine what it will be like, there's no way to prepare for the moment when you are ushered into the room to meet him. It was really something.

During the same visit, arrangements were made to rent the Sistine Chapel exclusively for PaineWebber brokers and their spouses for an entire afternoon and no other tourists were allowed. It is noteworthy that on a typical day, over 30,000 tourists visit this famous chapel to observe the beautiful work of Michelangelo on its ceiling.

In the early 1990's, my son's college buddy Nick asked if he could stay at my ranch down in Texas for an extended period of time. The pressures of living in New York City had gotten to him and he just wanted to retreat to a quiet place for some peace and solitude. The only living things there at the time besides the wild game were a few head of cattle. My ranch manager would visit the place every other day to check on things, but was neither sociable nor talkative, so I knew Nick would be completely alone.

I agreed, but warned him that he would be completely isolated. He assured me that that was exactly what he was looking for and flew down to Texas, but I had my doubts. Getting away from the fast pace of New York for a weekend was one thing, but being in the middle of nowhere with only yourself for company was quite another matter.

Sure enough, after three weeks Nick drove my '54 Chevy pick-up to the Garven Store six miles away and called Darvish. Nick was going crazy for lack of conversation. He said he had started talking to the cows, but they were not responding.

I laughed when my son told me this. "The time to worry is when the cows start talking back," I said.

Nick asked Darvish to come down and rescue him, so my son flew to Texas and went to the ranch. The two of them drove the old pick-up truck to Kerrville, but ran out of gas just outside of town. This is a common occurrence with newcomers in the area who aren't used to being more than five minutes away from the nearest 7-11.

Fortunately, they had brought a bottle of Bacardi 151% proof rum with them, which they poured into the tank. I guess they were celebrating the successful rescue of the city boy

from the clutches of the country. It was lucky they had not cel-
ebrated too hard and there was enough left in the bottle to get
them to Kerrville.

We took our final Caribbean vacation with Irv and three
other couples in the mid-nineties. This time, we stayed on Virgin Gorda in the British Virgin Islands. The name means "Fat
Virgin," which Christopher Columbus called it because he
apparently thought the island looked like a fat woman lying
on her side from one angle. I don't know where the 'virgin'
came from, unless he figured no one would sleep with an overweight woman.

It was a truly beautiful island, and we spent a lot of time
swimming and snorkeling the first day. On our second day,
another stockbroker friend sailed his yacht down from Miami
to join us, along with his son Matt, who was a struggling
actor. In the evenings we would go bar hopping and it turned
out to be another spectacular tip with our friends.

I was struck by Matt's intelligence, and remember thinking if he ever decided to give up show business, he would
make a fine stockbroker like his father. I had watched Matt
grow up, as he used to visit his father in our office fairly often
ever since he was a little boy.

It's a good thing he didn't, because a couple of years later
Matt Damon would win an Academy Award for best original
screenplay for Good Will Hunting, a movie he also starred in.

In 1994, my wife had started to develop arthritis and
could no longer tolerate the long cold winters of Boston. She
suggested we spend the winter months in a warmer climate.
Since I already had a ranch near San Antonio, Texas, it
seemed to make sense to go there during the winter.

So one day she flew to San Antonio with her foster-brother
Peiter, who was visiting us from England. Within days she rented
a house, and in October 1994 we moved in for the winter
months. Luckily PaineWebber had an office in San Antonio, so
it was fairly easy for me to conduct my business from there.

Six months later, just as we were getting ready to move back to Boston, Eliza asked me to look at a house for sale just down the street from our rental. It was a spacious one-story house on five acres and priced quite reasonably. We ended up buying it with the idea of spending the winters there. However, after a couple of months back in Boston, I compared our two properties. Looking at the hefty taxes I was paying in Boston, I decided to sell our house there and move to San Antonio permanently.

In the autumn of 1995, we bid farewell to our family and friends, had a moving company truck our household effects, and moved to Texas with our cat and dog.

My sister-in-law, who had become a real estate agent, helped us find an appropriate buyer for the Boston house. As it turned out, he was a developer with a lot of political contacts. He secured the necessary permits fairly quickly from a very unreceptive town hall, and ended up tearing our house down, filling the swimming pool, and building two enormous houses on the lot, which he then sold for many millions.

In San Antonio, we found a much more laid back lifestyle and friendly people to go with it. San Antonio is not a small town, but it had more open spaces and lacked the big city pressure and heavy traffic that Boston is known for, as well as the road rage and the notorious "big dig" that was so much a part of life in Beantown.

Of course I built a swimming pool in our new back yard. Texas is no place to be without a swimming pool. It really was a beautiful area. Every day we would watch whitetail deer graze on our property, and the sunsets were amazing.

We hired a Mexican lady to come once a week and clean the house, and a full time gardener to attend to the yard. Just mowing the lawn was a full day's work with a riding mower.

The move hardly affected my business at all since the bulk of it was conducted by telephone and fax. In fact, as time went by, I acquired quite a few locals to add to my already vast roster of clients.

A year later while Eliza and I were having dinner one evening at home, she told me that she was homesick for her native England. She also did not care for Texas at all because of the lack of culture.

But more than any of that, she admitted that she was tired of our marriage. We had been married thirty years by that time, and she was ready for a change.

For all of these reasons, she wanted to move back to her hometown of Brighton for good. To her credit, she did not just discount our many years together easily. I could see that it was a difficult decision for her even as I sensed her determination.

She gave me the option of going with her or staying behind, but I think we both knew what my answer would be. Since my business was based in the United States, and because I had just settled down in a new environment that was closer to my ranch, I chose to stay behind. She accepted my decision, and within weeks she had packed and left, leaving me to ponder the next phase of my life.

It was an odd time for me emotionally, and at first I had difficulty adjusting and dealing with the loneliness. Eliza had always been there for me, through good times and bad, and although we had our occasional rough patches, it was a successful marriage. She had been very supportive and instrumental in my drastic career change. I think we complimented each other well. I indulged her interest in the arts, and she put up with my ambitious business lifestyle.

After 35 years, it was strange to be without the woman who once paid my girlfriend two-and-a-half shillings to leave me for herself, but I would have to adjust.

Darvish was attending college in London at the time, and was quite upset about things. He urged us not to rush into a divorce, hoping that we might reconcile sometime in the future. But as my wife started to let other men into her life and I began to see other women, our son gradually accepted the fact that we were not going to get back together and adjusted his life accordingly.

He just wanted us to be happy.

I started to visit a local Italian restaurant which was staffed by a group of beautiful young waitresses. The food was fine, but the atmosphere was outstanding. I started to date a gorgeous twenty-six year-old blonde who was the 'senior' waitress, which I found amusing. After a few months I asked her if I could invite all the pretty waitresses out to a group dinner and she said she would arrange it.

I had become friendly with an Iranian who owned an Italian restaurant in San Antonio, and when I told him about the upcoming occasion, he suggested using the private room at his restaurant.

As I walked into the room that evening, there were nine gorgeous young women staring back at me. I thought I had died and gone to heaven.

We started with champagne and moved to wine, and by the time we left at mid-night we had gone through most of their best bottles. I invited them all to come to my place for a drink.

The great thing about pretty young girls is their spontaneity. Some of them jumped in the pool naked, while others just hung around the yard drinking until the wee hours of the night. My blonde girlfriend and a sexy brunette came to bed with me, but we were all so drunk that we just collapsed in bed and went to sleep.

I repeated this event a year later in the same restaurant, but this time half the girls were fresh faces, each more beautiful than the next. One of the new girls, a twenty-two year-old brunette, sat next to me at the restaurant and tried to get my attention most of the night. After dinner we all went back to my house and she pulled out a small box of cocaine and started snorting it. My blonde girlfriend told me she was an addict. It was such a shame, because that brunette was one of the most beautiful girls I had ever seen. Her aspiration was to go to Hollywood and become a movie star, but I knew she never would. Unlike Matt, there was nothing special about her besides her looks, and I could see that her addiction would probably take those from her eventually.

On page 109, I mentioned a little melodrama involving my swindling friends, the H brothers back in the 80's. Here is the continuing saga of that 734 acre tract of land in Georgetown that I purchased with three partners in 1980 and sold, with the help of the H brothers, in 1984.

At the time of the purchase, the owner had given us a twenty year first mortgage for $900,000, which required annual payments to him of $94,000. When we sold the land to the Texas matron in 1984, we gave her a wrap-around second lein for $1,400,000, which was to mature in ten years.

That note not only required paying the first lien holder $94,000 a year, but also paying us an additional $96,000 annually. Unbeknownst to me, the 6% commission that I paid the H brothers as broker's fee was split with the Texas lady, since they were in a 50/50 partnership.

This is what is affectionately known among thieves and scoundrels, as double dipping.

When the land was sold a year later to a Californian investor, the lady carried back a third wrap around note that not only covered the first and second lien payments, but paid $105,000 a year, which was again split between the her and her partners, the H brothers.

As I learned later, the California buyer stopped making payments to the seller after a few years, but continued payments to us and the first lienholder. I further learned that the Texas lady had elected to sell her half partnership interest with the brothers to the California investor at a substantial discount.

However, the H brothers insisted on holding onto their interest, and re-titled 425 acres of the property in the name of a Massachusetts-based corporation set up just for that purpose, which was executed without the knowledge of the Texas lady.

Basically, these guys were cheating everybody.

The annual payment of the second lien was punctually sent to us until its termination in 1994. But apparently, the payment to the first lienholder had stopped at some point, so I, along with all the other past investors, received a notice of foreclosure from the first lien holder during the summer of 1995.

The H brothers, penniless as usual, approached me asking for help. Even though they had screwed me time and again, being family, and with their mother pleading with me to help them and to save their land, I decided to step up to the plate and rescue them.

At that time the brothers showed me a letter of intent from a developer expressing interest in purchasing the land at the end of the year. Right from the outset, I told the family that my involvement was not for profit, but just to buy time until the land was sold. I further informed them that upon the sale of the land, all I wanted was to be repaid all my out-of-pocket expenses.

After that, I would bid them adieu and wish them luck.

Per my instructions, my attorney did a title search and discovered that since the Texas lady had not been properly notified of the foreclosure by the H brothers, there was still some ambiguity regarding her ownership interest, and that meant she was not completely out of the picture. When I confronted the H brothers, they said they would fly to Texas and meet with her and her attorney to clear all the uncertainties before the foreclosure date, which was set for September 3rd.

After returning from their meeting in Texas, they informed me they had been unable to reach a settlement but they would "guarantee" that by mid-September they would solve all their differences with the lady from Texas. They offered the same guarantee to cover back taxes amounting to over $43,000 that I had since discovered were overdue.

It is noteworthy that I had to bring this to their attention since they had conveniently omitted to mention it.

I went ahead and bought the outstanding balance of the first lien for $291,175 and paid the back taxes. Then I waited for action by the H brothers.

And I waited.

Not only were there no positive developments from their end by the original foreclosure date in September, but in December they informed me that their prospective buyer had walked away. A few days later I was sued by the Texas lady, claiming conspiracy to defraud in collusion with the H brothers.

Needless to say, I was getting very tired of this, and with my backing, various attempts were made by the H brothers to reach some kind of settlement, but to no avail. The entire ordeal was taking far too much of my time, energy, and focus from my extremely demanding business.

Finally, in early 1996 I had had enough. I broke off all professional relationships with the H brothers and instructed my attorney to proceed with foreclosure just to untangle me and get out of the mess. The H brothers of course filed for bankruptcy, a tactical delay to buy more time. In the meantime, all personal contacts had ceased and all communications were conducted through my attorney.

A couple of months later, they withdrew their bankruptcy petition and offered me $50,000 if I would delay the foreclosure for six months. I agreed, providing they would also present me with a settlement agreement with the Texas woman and indemnify me completely.

On June 3, 1996, my attorney was informed that they he should expect the signed settlement agreement plus the $50,000 at his office the next day.

It did not happen.

I finally foreclosed and ended up with a clear title after I settled with the Texas woman for $300,000.

It took me 10 years to find a suitable buyer for the 425 acre parcel, after which I voluntarily paid each brother $240,000 from the proceeds, even though by then I had ended all relationships with them.

They say if you want to get rid of someone sleazy, just loan them money and you'll never see them again.

After all those years of headaches and lies with the H brothers, that final payment was money well spent.

I was introduced to a few Iranians who had been living in San Antonio for a while, mostly businessmen, and joined their monthly social dinner. A couple of years later, one of them took me to a Texas Hold 'Em poker game he had been playing in for several years with a group of local men from all walks of life. They invited me to join, and from that day on I was hooked. I've been playing ever since.

I began to take a serious interest in poker, and became acquainted with a few locals who held regular Texas Hold 'Em games in their homes. I started to play two or three nights a week. On occasion, I would fly to Las Vegas for a 3-day stint and play 5-10 No Limit Poker at the Bellagio. I even participated in a few medium-sized tournaments and won two of them.

My fascination with games in general and poker in particular was not so much with the winning or losing, but with the stimulating challenges they offered, as well as the different characters and personalities you encountered. Poker players are often very strange and eccentric people, and a lot of fun to be around.

In my opinion, poker is one of the greatest entertainments in the world.

From the early years of my ranch ownership, I had invited a few friends and my two brothers, Reza and Ali, to join me during hunting season. I would often invite them all down for the weekend, and this pioneered the start of an annual reunion of old friends who grew up with together in Isfahan.

As the years went by, the number of 'old friends' who joined the reunion grew, primarily from word of mouth, and everyone started to look forward to this annual event. We would shoot deer and barbecue the meat, including the liver and other parts, drink beer and wine and just have a jolly good time. This tradition continues today, and in recent years the number of participants has grown to over two dozen.

It has been a long journey for us all from Isfahan to my ranch in Texas.

The day before the 2002 reunion and the opening of the deer season, it started to rain, and the downpour only got heavier as the day wore on. I had ordered a large stone table-top for an outdoor table at my ranch and asked my neighbor Ed if I could borrow his pick-up truck to haul it home. He instead offered to go with me to help. So at mid-day, we left, and with the help of a crane we picked up the two ton stone top, laid it in the back of the truck and drove to the ranch. We waited until dusk, but no one else showed up so we decided to drive back. I was concerned about the flooding at the ranch, and because of the heavy downpour the cell phones weren't working.

However, when we tried leaving, the rain had turned the exit road into a river and the motor flooded. Our heavy pick-up with the two ton stone table top in the back bed was carried on the surface of the water like a cork until we hit a fence and came to a stop. That was an unbelievable experience to be swept away in a vehicle like that, with absolutely no control. I hadn't felt such a sensation since my brother Reza and I flew down that mountain road on a bicycle driven by our opium-addled manservant as boys.

Once our truck lodged against the fence, we climbed on the roof and cat walked the fence until we reached solid ground.

We then walked a half mile until we got back to the county road. By then it was dark and we managed to flag down a passing truck. The driver offered to take us to Kerrville, a city 50 miles from my ranch to the west of San Antonio.

However, after we'd traveled just two miles, the road was so flooded that the police had shut down all traffic. We waited along with a number of other cars, primarily stranded hunters, for the water to subside before we could move again.

After six hours of waiting, finally the police removed the barricades and we were able to drive to Kerrville. This was a very good thing as we were all running out of beer and stories to tell.

We were dropped off at the YO Hotel a little after midnight, and much to our surprise, we found all our hunting buddies checked into the same hotel. Apparently on their way to the ranch they had been stopped on the other side of the flooded road and after hours of waiting they had returned and checked into the hotel for the night.

The next day we regrouped and returned to San Antonio and then went to the ranch a day later. Ironically enough, the flooded pick-up truck started right away and I was able to drive it back to San Antonio and deliver it, none the worse for wear, to its rightful owner. In the meantime, my resourceful manager had managed to pick up the heavy stone top with his bobcat and placed it on the table legs some 4 miles away from the drowned truck.

Darvish came to visit me from London and invited his college buddy Nick to fly down from New York and spend a few days with him in San Antonio. One afternoon, the two of them went out for a few beers. On the way back home, they pulled into a gas station to fill the Chevy Suburban, but being a little tipsy, they filled the 40-gallon tank with regular gas instead of diesel. Fortunately, they realized their mistake before attempting to start the car, avoiding damage to the engine.

They walked a couple of miles to a Home Depot, drinking all the way. I suppose if they had not been drinking in the first place, they might not have made the mistake in the first place.

But boys will be boys.

They bought a siphon pump and eight 5-gallon containers, walked the two miles back to the gas station, and spent the better part of the day in 102 degree heat pumping all the unleaded gas out of the Suburban and into the 5-gallon containers.

If they hadn't already been drinking, they sure could have used a drink after all that.

In 1997, my old friend Bijan who was living in Hawaii, brought to my attention an advertisement which he had seen in a travel magazine. It was placed by an outfit based in England called HERO (Historic Endurance Rally Organization), and invited individuals to participate in an organized drive from London to Cape Town, South Africa, scheduled for the fall of 1998.

The plan called for taking your own automobile and crew, and after paying certain fees to cover the costs, HERO would organize the route, reserve hotels and campsites, and assist with border crossings.

It sounded like I had found my next great adventure. I had been a student of history all my life and had read and familiarized myself with the history of most countries in the world and was anxious to visit some of the places I had read so much about. Most fascinating was the background of Egypt, China, South and Central America as well as Russia and Europe.

Throughout my life, it had always been my dream to drive around the world. I didn't know how or when I would accomplish that goal, but it was always there in the back of my mind. Maybe I would go awhile without thinking about it, but the dream never left me.

So when I saw the ad I was immediately excited and couldn't wait to get started. It was my fantasy come true and the trip of a lifetime.

I consulted my older brother Reza, who was living in Iran at the time, and my son Darvish, who was living in England. Much to my delight, they both expressed interest in taking part in this adventure. After signing up and two months before the start date, I drove my Chevy Suburban Diesel to Houston and dropped it off at the docks for shipment to London.

It was a good thing Darvish and Nick took that walk to Home Depot.

Joining me for the epic drive, besides Reza and Darvish, was my old friend Bijan who had originally brought the event to my attention.

In one of their many bulletins, HERO had suggested we all take some gifts for the locals in Africa, so I bought 20 small knives for the men and a bunch of underwear from Victoria's Secrets for the ladies. These gifts were received with utmost joy and pleasure.

I turned out to be a pretty popular driver with the locals.

You can't go wrong with blades and panties.

In order to prepare to visit all those counties, we had to obtain a number of visas. HERO provided a table indicating which countries required visas for U.S. citizens. Utilizing an agency in Los Angeles that specialized in this kind of work, they forwarded all the necessary applications to us, and after filling them up and returning them with the appropriate photos and fees, our paperwork was processed. It took over a month before the visas were secured for all four of us, so I was quite grateful for the excellent organization by the sponsors.

We were all very excited about this great adventure. On October 24, 1998, a cold, drizzly day, a total of 84 automobiles from all over the world were flagged off from the starting gate at London's Dockland Wharf, and left at one-minute intervals starting at 8:00 AM.

A large crowd of friends and families, as well as media was on hand to see us off. A number of reporters and photographers had gathered to record this historic event and the start of the 12,000 mile drive from London to Cape Town.

About half of the participating automobiles were classic vehicles, ranging from a 1917 Simplex to a 1923 Bentley to a 1947 Allard. Some of them were convertibles, which made driving and navigating in rain and snow and dust far more difficult, but the participants claimed it represented a bigger challenge.

After loading up the automobiles on the train in Folkestone, my old college town, and crossing the English Channel, we drove through Belgium and spent the first night at Spa. On the way there we got lost a few times and had to ask for directions. Back then all the navigation systems and GPS devices were just starting to appear on the market and we weren't sophisticated enough to own any of them.

The older I get the more I marvel at all the modern conveniences that make things so much easier nowadays.

At the time of our initial registration in London, we had been given a road-book, which to us looked like Egyptian Hieroglyphs or something, and we paid no attention to it during our entire first day of driving. But before dinner at our hotel in Spa, we approached a HERO official and asked if she would go over the many signs and notations in the road-book and show us how to use it.

We learned that each page showed in great detail every mile of the route we were to follow, down to the turn, detour, bridge, highway, street, road, and path. It was our 'Bible' for the trip, and had been painstakingly put together by the HERO staff. These road-books were referred to as "Tulips." Once again, the organization was quite impressive.

Singapore - Macau 2009

Day Five: Ferringhi - Rayavadee

Section 5.3: Chang Long - DF 5 Rayavadee   173.1 km

Row No	Interval km	Section km	Interval miles	Section miles	Tulip symbol	Landmark/instruction	Waypoint
1	0.00	0.00	0.00	0.00		Welcome to Thailand End of Section 5.2, start of Section 5.3	WP 5.05 Zero trip N6 31.485 E100 25.097
2	0.00	2.03	0.00	1.26		Detour through customs shed Route survey crew were not stopped	
3	10.45	12.48	6.49	7.76		To gantry SP Hat Yai A2	
4	3.11	15.59	1.93	9.69		Giant Buddha	
5	6.10	21.69	3.79	13.48		Fuel	
6	8.47	30.16	5.26	18.74		In Ban Khlong Ngae - avoid R lane Caltex	
7	21.27	51.43	13.22	31.96		Filter L before & flyover SP Rte 43 Phatthalung	WP 5.06 N6 58.444 E100 28.745
8	0.35	51.78	0.22	32.18		PTT - plenty of fuel on this road	
9	5.45	57.23	3.39	35.57		SP Rte 43 Phatthalung (⇐ Airport)	
10	1.46	58.69	0.91	36.48		SP Rte 43 Phatthalung (Cross Rte 4 SP ⇒ Hat Yai ⇐ Satun) Fairly busy free flowing dual carriageway	
11	22.54	81.23	14.01	50.48		SP Rte 4 Phatthalung (SP ⇐ Rte 4 Satun)	

Page of directions from the Road-Book

4

Sample Page from the Tulip

Our route took us through Germany, Austria, and Croatia, with an overnight stop in Bucharest, Romania. The doorman at our hotel in Bucharest politely offered to arrange for young ladies or boys sent to our rooms, but we declined. The next day as we were leaving the city in early hours of the morning, we saw hundreds of prostitutes lined up on either side of the highway, catering primarily to the truckers.

It looked like a casting call for some low budget porn film.

Crossing the border into Turkey took several hours but we finally entred the country and spent the night in Istanbul before continued on to Cappadocia, a region in the central part of the country famous for its beauty. There are rock formations known as "fairy chimneys," and hundreds of ancient rock dwellings, many carved into the hillside thousands of years ago. Some of them are still utilized for such things as coffee houses and artist studios.

Houses carved into the mountains at Cappadocia

The next day we entered Syria and visited Krak des Chevalier, a gigantic stone fortress built on top of a hill a thousand years ago by the Crusaders and occupied during their visits.

In Jordan we swam at the Dead Sea, which was so saturated with salt that one could not submerge without a lot of effort. We floated in the afternoon sun as the water lapped across our chests. Darvish covered himself there with the local

The majestic Krak des Chevalier

mud, which dried quickly and was supposed to have healing qualities. He looked like the Creature from the Black Lagoon before he scrubbed off.

The next day we paid a visit to Petra, a city the Romans carved into the face of a mountain about two thousand years ago. It had a 'street,' carved into the slope of Mount Hor, lined on one side with government buildings, which were actually large cavities in the rock. The Treasury and Amphitheatre were on one side and dwellings on the other. It was truly spectacular. The name Petra is Greek for rock, and city was named by the BBC as one of forty places on earth one should see before they die.

Once you actually see it, you know exactly what they meant.

We spent one night at Aqaba before entering Israel, where we were met at the border by several military vehicles with mounted machine guns that carried Israeli soldiers who escorted us all across their country to the Egyptian border for security and safe journey.

Finally, after driving through the Suez Canal, we entered Africa, and after spending the night at the beautiful resort city of Sharm el-sheikh on the Egyptian coast, we reached the city

The Treasury at Petra

of Hurghada, which is the second largest city in Egypt and a big tourist attraction in a country filled with them.

We stayed there for a couple of days while waiting for HERO to organize an airlift over Sudan because the U.S.

Embassy had just been bombed and terrorist activity made it dangerous for our group to drive through.

Since we had a couple of rest days there, we took a bus trip to Luxor and visited the Karnack Temple Complex, a vast area filled with the ruins of temples, giant columns, and other structures, including the Great Temple of Amun. The construction of the temple started some 3500 years ago and after 1000 years of construction it was left incomplete because of the invasion by Alexander the Great of Greece.

Columns inside Karnak Temple

We then went to the Valley of the Kings and visited some of the Pharaohs' tombs. The wall paintings inside the tombs remained intact and their bright colors seemed to glow in the dim light. Taking photos was prohibited because of possible flash damage to the artwork, but the security guard just walked over, asked for $2, and told us to take all the pictures we wanted.

On flight day, all the autos were loaded onto two giant Russian Antonov air freight planes, some of the world's largest, while the passengers took Egypt Air to Entebbe airport in Kampala, Uganda, the airport made famous around the world when Israeli Defense Forces raided the main terminal in 1976 after an Air France flight originating in Tel Aviv had been hijacked and forced to land there.

We were now in what I like to call the real Africa, surrounded by exotic wildlife.

After driving by Mt. Kilimanjaro in Kenya, we made a stop at Lake Bogoria to look at the thousands of pink pelicans that nest there.

Every day brought another extraordinary experience. We were having the time of our lives.

Pink Pelicans on Lake Bogoria, Kenya

We then stopped in Nairobi and visited a Maasai Village and watched the locals in their colorful outfits in action at a cattle auction. A group of teenage boys with painted faces approached our car and we were told that the designs on their faces signified that they had been recently circumcised.

Imagine walking around with that news on your face!

Maasai Village in Kenya

Our next overnight stop was at the Ngorongoro Crater in a conservation area in Tanzania, where we saw a wide variety of wild animals like lions, rhinos, elephants, and wildebeests. The drive to the crater was 80 Km away over some very rough dirt roads, and took us 3 1/2 hours.

While driving through an African village, we saw a group of young boys chasing a wooden bicycle. At my son's request, we stopped and he asked them if he could ride it. They were only too happy to see a tourist take an interest in their home-made bike.

After satisfying himself that it was 'ridable,' Darvish bargained with the boys and ended up buying the bike for $2. We tied it on the roof rack and had it shipped with our car back to Texas. It is made entirely of wood, including the wheels, and is now on display at my house in San Antonio. It's quite a conversation piece.

On our way to Cape Town, we made many stops and bought quite a few pieces of African-made jewelry and hand-made canes as souvenirs. In one village, I even persuaded a young girl who was selling necklaces to take her own necklace off and sell it to me for my girlfriend.

In Namibia, we stopped at Livingstone's Village and then proceeded to our overnight stop at Namutoni, where late that night at a watering hole adjacent to our campsite, we saw several lions making a meal out of some gazelles who had come to drink. It was another amazing, once-in-a-lifetime experience.

At the Zambian border we were greeted by a dancing group of local women in traditional costumes, and all along the roads we saw young boys offering to sell monkeys, ostrich eggs and other African animals, all illegally.

The streets of Africa were teeming with entrepreneurs.

When we reached the magnificent Victoria Falls, we were again greeted by local dancers in colorful dresses. I wonder what it would be like if everywhere you went in the United States people greeted you like that.

Finally, on December 1, we reached Cape Town, South Africa and the end of the Adventure Drive. After a well-publicized finish line ceremony, we all flew home while arrangements were being made by HERO to ship our automobiles back home.

Cape of Good Hope

Wherever available, I purchased a sticker representing the country we were in and stuck it on the back of our car. By the end of the journey, the back of the Suburban was completely covered with colorful stickers.

Before embarking on this adventure, I had bought a two door Chevy Tahoe for the drive. But as we got closer to the departure date, I realized that the car was not that practical and we needed a four-door vehicle with more interior space. So I traded it in for a 4-door Diesel Chevy Suburban with heavy-duty suspension and larger rims and tires. I also had some work done on the Chevy Suburban and had a small refrigerator installed with a heavy-duty roof rack custom made for it. To access it, I had a special removable ladder constructed. In addition, I had two folding seats with seat belts designed and bolted to the roof rack.

On occasion, Darvish and Bijan would sit on the roof while I was driving through scenic areas.

When the car was returned from South Africa, there were a number of items missing from it. Half the contents were stolen, including a case of South African wine. Even the floodlights around the roof rack had been stripped.

When I reported this to the Marine Insurance Co. in England, they asked for evidence. I sent them before and after photos of the car, but they told me that they had no idea where the theft had taken place and used all kind of excuses not to honor their coverage.

The next year, I bought a Ferrari Maranello 550 and when the Ferrari Club invited all the owners to a racetrack in College Station, Texas to race their vehicles for a weekend I signed up. Darvish and a couple of his old friends from Boston joined me and we drove my Ferrari around the track for two full days. It was a thrilling experience. Only when you open up on a track like that do you realize the full potential of a performance car like a Ferrari. It was mind boggling.

That same year I was introduced to a charming 26 year old African princess from Ethiopia who was residing in San Antonio at that time. She was extremely attractive, well educated and brought up in a royalty fashion. We dated for a while before she moved to Houston to pursue higher education.

During a routine check up in 2002, my doctor informed me that my sugar level has risen and recommended that I see a specialist. After extensive tests, I was diagnosed with hereditary Diabetes and was told to start by taking the dietary class offered by the clinic. When I walked into the class at 7 pm. One evening there were eight lady students each weighing an average of 350 lbs. They took one look at my athletic figure weighing only 138 lbs. and asked if I was in the right class.

During the session the teacher started to talk about exercise and the ladies panicked. She said all you need to do is walk 20 minutes a day but the ladies could not tolerate that. One of them said she backs out of her driveway and drives across the road to a convenient store located across from her house and after shopping she just backs her car up to her driveway.

No wonder they weighed so much and had serious diabetic problems. As for me, I have taken the medications prescribed and along with vigorous daily exercises, managed to kept my blood sugar well under control.

Just prior to embarking on the African Adventure Drive, I met a charming 31 year-old Iranian girl named Lida living in Pasadena, California and started dating her. At the time she was attending California State College studying computer science.

I would fly to LA and spend a weekend with her and she would reciprocate by coming to my house in San Antonio, Texas once in a while.

The 1999 Chairman Council trip with PaineWebber was held in Switzerland, and I took my new girlfriend Lida. The opening night dinner was arranged at the thousand year-old Chillon Castle right on the edge of Lake Geneva. The commute to and from the castle was by boat.

During the dinner, a 60 year-old woman went to the bathroom and did not return. After some 45 minutes, her husband got quite worried and went looking for her, only to find that she had locked herself in a 1000 year-old bathroom, and despite knocking and yelling, had been unable to get anyone's attention.

Chillon Castle

VII.
2000's

San Antonio -The World
"Exploring the Globe to the End"

DURING A VISIT to Iran in 1998, my son fell in love with my best friend's 18 year-old daughter, and they dated each other for three years before getting married.

My father and the bride's father had spent a lifetime together as friends. so our family backgrounds were no mystery to anyone. They were quite well established in Isfahan.

The happy couple had a great mixed reception in March of 2001 in Tehran, and soon after they settled down in Brighton, England where I bought a waterfront condo for them as a wedding gift.

I should explain that in Iranian weddings and under the Islamic law, men and women are not permitted to comingle. They celebrate such an occasion in two separate quarters, one for men one for women. However, a lot of people do not follow those rules, and in my son's case, the bride's father had paid off the local police not only to look the other way, but also to keep an eye out and protect the event from intruders.

The wedding was conducted in true Islamic fashion at a registry in Tehran, but the reception was organized and held in the parking floor under her parent's condominium tower. There was great food and a live band playing mostly western songs to which people danced well into the early hours of the morning.

Alcohol was served discretely in their kitchen condo upstairs and by invitation only.

It's better sometimes not to push one's luck.

In 2000, the Chairman's Council members were taken to Paris as a reward. I again attended with Lida, and they put us up at the George V Hotel, which is a famous five star hotel and one of the finest in Paris. My brother Ali, who had followed in my footsteps and joined PaineWebber in 1984 also qualified to come to Paris with his wife.

The first night they arranged a gala dinner for everyone at Versailles Palace. It was a spectacular event and one of the best dinners ever.

Dinner at Versailles

My son, who was living in London at the time, took the train and joined us in Paris for a few days. I told the management my son would be staying in our room with us, and not knowing his age, the maid left an infant tee shirt on his bed as a welcoming gift, which gave us all a good laugh.

It was during this trip that I informed PaineWebber senior management of my decision to retire later that same year when I reached the age of 60. Upon my return to San Antonio, I made all the necessary arrangements to pass on my clients to my younger brother Ali, who was a Sr. Vice President and operated out of the Wellesley office in Massachusetts.

Soon after my retirement in the fall of 2000, the stock market boom caused by the explosion in technology and Internet came to an abrupt end, and prices started to drop from their lofty levels. Two of my former clients, who also happened to be good Iranian friends living in San Antonio, complained to PaineWebber about the decrease in the value of their portfolios, and sought damages.

They felt that since I was no longer there, maybe the firm would make restitution. I felt betrayed by this and broke all relationships with them.

Prior to the turn of the century, one of the greatest concerns had been possible computer and system glitches for the millennium, but as we entered the year 2000, everything went quite smoothly, much to the relief of everyone.

Ironically, within weeks of my retirement, PaineWebber was bought out by UBS, which further secured my financial independence since I owned a large number of PaineWebber shares.

I had been very fortunate in my career. I worked hard, but I had also been in the right place and the right time quite often. They say a hard-working man makes his own luck, so I guess that was true in my case.

In September of 2001, a year after I retired, my son was visiting me in San Antonio when early in the morning of the 11th I received a call from my brother Ali, urging me to turn on the TV. I watched the events taking place in New York City with horror like so many others as the second plane hit the North Tower of the World Trade Center.

For a while it was total confusion and hard to figure out what was going on and what had caused all this and, and we were glued to the TV all day trying to grasp the significance of the attacks.

After my retirement, it was my intention to focus on travel. I wanted to see as much of the world as possible. It was right around then that HERO announced their next Adventure Drive, this time through South America and scheduled for the fall of 2001.

I shipped the same Chevy Suburban Diesel that had taken us three years earlier from London to Cape Town, to Rio de Janeiro in Brazil where the drive was scheduled to start. Rio de Janeiro is a great city with some of the most attractive beaches on the planet. The landmarks like Sugarloaf Mountain and the giant statue of Christ called Corcovado make it a unique place to visit.

I modified the car, removing the refrigerator and replacing the roof rack with a lighter weight rack and shortening the access ladder. This time, my crew consisted of my brother Reza, my cousin Bahram (my zoologist uncle's son) and Bahram's brother-in-law Michael, an Englishman who lived in Cornwall, England.

During this drive, like the prior one, there were a mix of 4X4's and classic cars that included a 1936 Buick, a 1965 Ferrari 330 GT, and a 1960 Aston Martin DB 4.

On October 6, 2001, a total of 107 automobiles from all over the world were flagged off at Fort Copacabana in Rio to start a 15,000 mile drive throughout South America that would last 60 days.

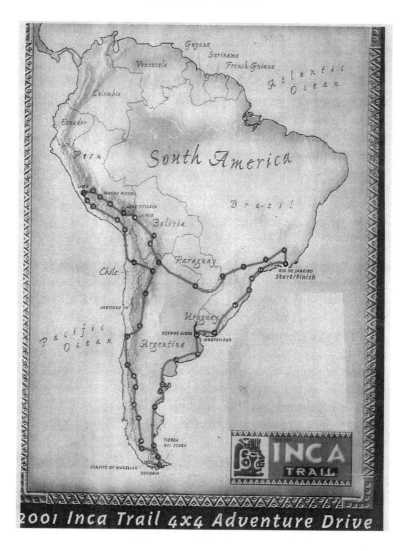

2001 Inca Trail 4x4 Adventure Drive

After departing Rio, our first stop was Iguazu Falls, which is a spectacular series of 275 drops, the highest of which is the Devil's Throat at 269 feet.

We then drove to the silver mining town of Potosi after crossing into Bolivia and visited the cliffs just outside Sucre, where thousands of Dinosaur footprints are clearly visible.

Rio de Janeiro

Classic Cars

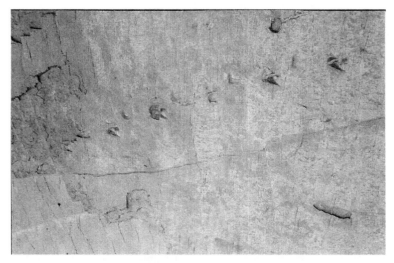

Dinosaur Footprints

We entered Peru after taking the ferry across Lake Titicaca, and continued on to Cusco for two days of rest. On the way we made brief stops at the Inca ruins of Ollantaytambo and Sacsayhuaman.

During our second day of rest in Cusco, we took the train and visited the famous village of Machu Picchu, which, according to the historians, was built on top of the mountain in 1438 and abandoned sometime after the Spanish conquest. No one has been able to figure out what happened to the inhabitants ever since.

Arriving in Lima a few days later, we stayed at the massive El Pueblo resort for another day's rest. The following evening, the locals put on a spectacular performance for us in the Plaza Principal of the resort. The colorful costumes and the dancing were fantastic.

On our way out of Peru, we stopped and spent half a day visiting the Nazca Lines. These were giant animals and geometric designs drawn in the desert, visible only from the air. We went up in a small airplane to get a clear view of them. A number of the participants went up in groups of four to look at them. The lines were thought to have been made by the Paracas and Nazca culture from 900 BC to 600 AD. It was quite a thing to see.

Ruins of Machu Picchu

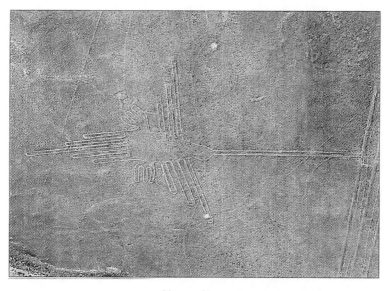

Nazca Lines

The next day we crossed over into Chile and drove all day across the Chilean desert, where we were told it had not rained in 70 years. We reached Chuquicamata Township, which is the home of the largest opencast copper mine in the world. The hole was 8 kilometers by 4.5 kilometers and 1 kilometer deep.

That was one big hole.

After exploring Chile for a few days, we entered Argentina. After passing Flamingo Soda Lake and some amazing rock formations on Sierra de Malanzan, we re-entered Chile and started ascending the Andes. By mid-day we reached Aconcagua at 22,825 feet (6959 meters), which is the highest point in the Americas.

Next, we proceeded to Lanin Volcano, Punta Panoramica, and Llao Llao Lake, where we saw a variety of colorful, tropical wild flowers along the road.

One night we camped out at Estonicia Suyai, where the locals barbecued twenty-five whole lambs for our dinner, which I supplemented by cooking a large pot of rice that we shared with everyone. I had taken a large bag of Basmati rice with us for such an occasion.

BBQ Lamb in Argentina

As we approached the southern part of Argentina, we visited the spectacular Perito Moreno Glacier. We took a boat ride and got close to the ice cliffs, which rose hundreds of feet above the surface of the water. Every now and then a large piece would break off and collapse into the water with an ear-splitting crash.

Perito Moreno Glacier

A few days later, we took a ferry to the Straits of Magellan and onto Tierra del Fuego before reaching Ushuaia, the southernmost town in Argentina. The signpost on the waterfront read, "End of the Earth.

Shortly after that we headed north along the eastern coast of Argentina, and after a few days we reached the Petrified Forest National Monument. It was an eerie place, like a deserted, arid, science fiction-type landscape. Further north we reached the penguin colony of Punto Tambo, where thousands of penguins congregate along the shore.

Farther north we saw whales and elephant seals at Valdes Peninsula, and later on our drive we visited Juan Manuel Fangio's hometown of Balcarce. We saw the auto collection of the legendary race car driver, and tested our vehicles on his private autodromo.

When we arrived in Buenos Aires, the British Ambassador threw a great reception at his private garden in our honor.

At our overnight stop in Paranagua, the locals preformed a fandango dance for us at the Maracado Café, and on November 30th, we reached Rio de Janeiro and crossed the finish line for the termination of that year's Adventure Drive.

In 2004, HERO put together a drive through China and Tibet that was limited to 4x4s only because of rough roads and high altitude in the Himalayas.

This time, Reza and I, along with two Texans from El Paso, joined 31 other vehicles to cover the 5,600 mile (9000 km) drive. This trip, which was originally scheduled to take place in the fall of 2003, had to be delayed by 6 months because of the SARS Flu epidemic in China. Prior to the start of our drive, Reza and I spent a couple of days in Beijing visiting Tiananmen Square and the Forbidden City which was established between 1406 and 1420 by the Yongle Emperor, who commanded battalion of up to a million laborers.

It was called the Forbidden City because it was off limits to outsiders for 500 years. During that time, the admission price for an outsider would have been instant death. It's the world's largest and best-preserved imperial palace complex, and one of the most alluring and magnificent Chinese treasures. The complex is surrounded by a moat and has 9,999 rooms, one short of the number that ancient Chinese believe represented divine perfection. It signified the distant and unapproachable emperor. For five centuries, the palace functioned as an administrative center of the country as well as being the pleasure home of the emperors who were served by thousands of eunuchs, servants and maids.

No matter what the culture or period, it's good to be the king.

We then went on to the Summer Palace, which is a sprawling imperial encampment of temples, pavilions, and halls set in a park around the vast, man-made Kunming Lake. The Summer Palace was conceived in the 12th century, and was once a playground for the imperial court. The royalty went there to elude the insufferable summer heat that roasted the Forbidden City.

The Gate of Supreme Harmony at Forbidden City

We also paid a visit to Maoliando Street, lined with thousands of tea shops and offering what seemed like as many varieties of tea.

We picked up our vehicle from the warehouse just outside of Beijing and went through the formalities of registering and collecting our road-books. By this time I was an old pro at all this stuff. We were also got our Chinese Driver's Licenses.

My Chinese Driver's License

The Adventure Drive officially started on April 28th at the Great Wall of China, where each car was flagged off at the starting gate. That was a pretty spectacular way to begin.

Great Wall of China

Heading west, we arrived at Pingyao, one of China's three well-preserved ancient cities (the other two being Xian and Jingzhou). With a history of over 2700 years, the city stands out as the best preserved of the walled cities in China. It is a marvelous example of Chinese Han cities during the Ming and Qing dynasties, and it unfolds as an outstanding historical development in terms of its culture, society, economy and religion.

The city is nicknamed Turtle City, with two gates on the south and north representing the head and the tail of the turtle and four gates on the east and west, representing the four legs. The two doors on the south and on the north stand opposite to each other, like the head of a turtle extending out, and two wells just beyond the southern gate are like the turtle's two eyes. Along the wall, there are platforms 50 meter apart, 3000 crenels on the outer wall and 72 watchtowers with battlements.

The city wall was first built during Zhou Dynasty (11th Century-256 BC), and was expanded in 1370, the third year of the reign of Ming Emperor Hongwu.

Ancient Wall at Pingyao

A few days later we arrived at the Dragon Gate Grottos (aka Longmen Shiku), which housed many images, paintings, and statues carved into the cliff walls on the banks of Yi He River. It is one of those treasured houses of stone in China that date back to the time when the northern Wei Dynasty moved its capital to Luoyang around 493 AD.

There are 2345 niches, over a hundred thousand sculptures, and some 2800 pieces of stones bearing inscriptions on both the east and west side of the river.

Statues carved into the cliff walls at the Dragon Gate Grottoes

Upon arrival in Xian, we took a day to visit the amazing Terracotta Warriors that Emperor Qin Shi Huang had buried about 200 B.C. He wanted to take his entire army with him for protection into the afterlife when he died. He was the first emperor to establish a centralized state and abolish the feudal system, and to further unify the country, Emperor Qin standardized the system of weights and measures, handwriting into small seal script, and standardized the width of carriage axles to six feet.

Apparently, on March 29, 1974, when local farmers of Xi Yang Village were drilling a series of wells in search of water, some pottery fragments and ancient bronze weapons were discovered. With help from the government, an archaeological team arrived at the site and began their explorations and excavations. So far, over 1000 terra-cotta warriors and horses have been restored and are on display. We saw the kneeling Archers, the Horse, and the Chariot in incredible preserved condition. Emperor Qin died at the age of 50, and his tomb, about 1 1/2 Km. from his warriors, has not yet been opened.

Terracotta Warriors

Heading towards the Himalayas, we stopped at Ta'er Monastery, which is one of the most significant Tibetan monasteries outside Tibet. It is one of the six Yellow Hat Sect Lamaseries, and is revered for its association with the founder of the Yellow Hat Sect Tsongkhapa, who was born in the 14th century. Its cluster of buildings include a fine temple roofed with over 3000 kg (6614 lbs.) of gold tiles, several stupas, and a hall containing Yak butter sculptures, a historic Tibetan art form which represented many hours of hard work by Buddhist monks. They were colorfully painted and kept under glass containers.

Yak butter sculptures under glass

The monastery, which was at an elevation of 6,585 feet, housed more than 700 monks. It is an honor for a family's first son to become a monk. Inside the temple, it is customary to walk in a clockwise direction for religious reasons.

In the town of Golmud, the street was lined with locals playing Mah Jonng and snooker on the sidewalk. Wearing masks to protect them from SARS was commonplace.

On our way to Shigatse, Tibet, we passed a number of stupas, including Chorter Rang-Po. We also saw a number of Yaks wearing prayer flags while plowing in the fields.

Once in Shigatse, we went to the local outdoor bazaar, and after an exhaustive amount of bargaining with the local women, we bought some handicrafts, including some beautiful jewelry. We also paid a visit to Tashilhunpo Monastery, which occupied 70,000 square meters and was founded by Ge Dun Drupa, the first Dali Lama, in 1447.

There, we saw many statues of Buddha covered with gold and a massive, 85 foot high beatific effigy of Maitreya, the future Buddha.

The Tashilhunpo Monastery, with its colorful wall paintings, is the largest in 'Back of Tibet,' and home to Panchen Lamas. The largest is in Llasa, 'the front of Tibet.'

The present Panchen Lama was nominated by the Chinese government, and lives in Beijing. The Dalai Lama, who was the head of the Yellow Hat Sect of Tibetan Buddhism, fled Tibet in 1959 for India after the Chinese invasion. While the Dalai Lama is the spiritual and temporal ruler of the land, the Panchen Lama is a physical incarnation of the Antiabha Buddha, and enjoys successive incarnations, just like the Dalai Lama.

After entering the Himalayas and spending a night at New Tingri in Tibet, we got up very early the next day, drove into the mountains for an hour, and witnessed the most stunning view of the Himalayas, with Everest at the center with a halo of clouds over it. With the low early morning sun casting its cool light and long shadows, the mountain scenery was particularly awe-inspiring.

Mt. Everest at Sunrise

After absorbing that early morning spectacle, we drove to Mt. Everest base camp at 16,000 feet above sea level and watched several groups of climbers preparing to make an assault at the peak the next day. Because of the thin air and lack of oxygen at that level, our vehicles struggled very slowly up the rugged terrain.

We arrived at Lhasa, the capitol of Tibet a few days later and were greeted with a welcoming ceremony by the locals. We visited the Potala Palace, the former residence of the Dalai Lama, which had been turned into a museum. The palace, which is a typical Tibetan structure, was first built in the 7th century, and then rebuilt in 1645 by Desi Sangye Gyalso, and it included the white Palace. In 1690 Desi constructed the 13 story Red Palace in the center of Potala to hold the golden Stupa Tomb of the fifth Dalai Lama, along with many precious shrines and relics. The palace has 1000 rooms. Most of its treasures have been removed by the Chinese government and taken to Beijing.

Potala Palace

While shopping in Lhasa, we stumbled across a local artist who specialized in painting portraits of various Tibetans. We were so impressed by her work that Reza and I each bought one of her pieces.

Over the next few days, we worked our way out of Tibet and drove back to China, and were caught in a snowstorm just outside Deqen. As we descended, the weather changed dramatically and we started to see spring flowers everywhere. After driving over some rough, gravel roads, we stopped at Zhongdian Monastery and at Tiger Leaping Gorge.

In Lijang, we visited the old part of town, which was occupied primarily by Naxis, the descendants of ethnically Tibetan Qiang Tribes that lived until recently in matrilineal families. Since local rulers were always male, it was not truly matriarchs, but women seem to run the show and maintain their hold over the men with flexible arrangements of love affairs.

The Naxis have their own traditions, art, and music, and their costumes were extremely colorful.

Naxi ladies having lunch

There were a myriad of small streets where we found a variety of artisans in their shops. We visited the Mu Family Mansion and pagoda where Mu, the former Naxi chieftain, ruled like a King.

When we reached Dali, we visited the three pagodas and the Chongsheng Temple, which was also converted to a museum.

As we drove east and away from Tibet, the weather started to improve, and we gradually entered the tropical regions in southeastern China. We reached the breathtaking Huangguoshu Falls on May 24th, and then for the balance of the drive we passed by a number of fishing villages and rice paddies. It was a relaxing way to end the adventure.

On May 27th we reached Schenzhen where the drive officially terminated. After a spectacular finishing ceremony, we were bused to Hong Kong, and the next day we flew home.

Performers at the Finishing Ceremony

The next Adventure Drive organized by HERO was through Central America in 2006. My Chevy Suburban had gotten too old, so I replaced it with a new 2007 Chevy Tahoe 4-wheel drive. GM had stopped production of diesel cars, so

I had to settle for a gasoline-operated vehicle. It should be noted that diesel engines are much more durable and require much less maintenance than gasoline-operated automobiles. They are also far more suitable for long adventure drives. Reza and I, having three prior drives under our belts, decided to do this drive by ourselves without adding any other crew members.

I drove the vehicle to Los Angeles where I hooked up with Reza and we drove down to La Jolla to spend the night. One of the participants of the 2001 South American drive, a renowned physician, had thrown a party at his beautiful house and invited about a dozen participants of the current drive for drinks and dinner. The hospitality was beyond all our expectations. Once you've done an Adventure Drive, you're almost like family. The experience bonds you to the other participants because it's like no other experience.

The next day we drove to Ensenada, Mexico to start our adventure.

On November 7, 2006, a total of 26 vehicles, all 4-wheel drive, started a 7,000 miles (11,200 km) journey from Ensenada, Mexico to Panama City a month later.

Driving south through Baja, we rested for a day in Cabo San Lucas before taking the ferry across to Los Mochis. We made a stop at the historic city of El Fuerte and visited a number of Colonial buildings, including the Municipal Palace.

We then continued on and stopped overnight at Divisadero, which sits on the rim of the Copper Canyon. The next day on the way to Zacatecas, we stopped at Villa del Oeste, a movie set where many a Hollywood western had been made.

In Zacatecas, one of the most beautiful cities in Mexico, we stayed at the Hotel Quinta Real, which is built around an old bull fighting ring. In the evening, the locals brought a band and we followed them through the streets with Tequila carried in large jags and served constantly to everyone by the members of the hotel staff. It turned out to be quite a lively evening.

When we arrived in Guanajuato, we spent a full day visiting this historic town with its beautiful buildings, including the Juarez Theatre.

Theatre Juarez in Guanajuato

Guanajuato was one of the first areas in Mexico colonized by the Spanish in 1520, and was built over a rich vein of silver discovered by Juande Tolosa in 1546. This and other mines in the vicinity attracted a large population. Their silver and that from Potosi, Peru was coined as pieces of eight and transported around the world by Spanish treasure fleets and Manila Galleons. It was this silver that paid for the wars of the Spanish Empire. Its Colonial architecture is well preserved, along with over thirty-five old churches. It's very European in appearance.

On November 17th, we reached Mexico City and spent the next two days exploring this magnificent and heavily populated city. One day a few of us hired a minivan and a guide who took us to see the Teotihuacan Pyramids. Our guide explained that the city of Teotihuacan dates back to 150 BC, and is the archeological site most visited in Mexico. Between 1 AD and 250 AD, the ceremonial core was completed, including the Pyramids of the Sun, the Moon and Calle de los Muertos.

Trading relationships were established with Monte Alban in Oaxaca and the gulf coast, and a major expansion of population and housing occurred between 250-450 AD, when as many as 200,000 inhabitants occupied at least 2000 houses. The prosperity continued to 650 AD, and around this time it was the sixth largest city in the world.

Three hundred years later it was found virtually abandoned. Because of a major fire in 650 AD, the population gradually moved to other growing cities, and by the time the Aztecs arrived, Teotihuacan was little more than an ancient ruin.

The basilica, the Cathedral Metropolitan, the Palacio National and the Blacio de Bellos Artes were of great interest.

Throughout the city, murals by the famous artist Diego Rivera, portraying the sufferings of the Aztecs at the hands of the Spanish, as well as his other works, were plastered on the walls.

On the way to Acapulco, we made a stop in the picturesque town of Taxco, which sits atop a hill, and visited its main square with a magnificent Colonial Church. When we reached Acapulco, we made like typical tourists and just laid out on the beach for a day before driving to Lagunas de National Park, where we took a boat ride down the lagoon and admired a wide variety of wildlife.

A few days later, after stopping briefly at the Aqua Azul and Misol-Ha waterfalls, we stopped overnight at Palenque, and the next day visited the splendid temples there built by the Mayans.

Vast, mysterious and enchanting, the ruined city of Palenque is considered to be the most beautifully conceived of the Mayan city-states, and one of the greatest archeological sites in the world. Nestled amidst steep and thickly forested hills, the ruins are frequently shrouded in lazy mist. A rushing brook meanders through the city center, and from the temple summits there are stupendous views over an immense coastal plain.

Scattered pottery shards show that the site was occupied from as early as 300 BC, and that most of the buildings were constructed between the 7th and 10th centuries AD. While the ruins have received some of the most extensive reconstruction efforts of any Mayan sites, only 34 structures of an estimated 500 scattered around the area have been uncovered.

The temple has three limestone panels with hieroglyphic inscriptions and stucco reliefs. Inside, there is an imposing funeral crypt decorated with bas relieves where the sarcophagus of Lord Sun Shield (Pakai) is located. Pakai ruled Palenque from 615 to 683 AD. There is also a large central scene that portrays his death and shows the celestial heavens and various deities, symbols, and signs that together represent a synthesis of the Mayan cosmic vision.

Piercing the dark green forests are soaring pyramids, towers, and sprawling temple complexes, which used to be painted in rainbow of pastels. Hidden deeply in the jungle, the ruins' existence was unknown until 1773.

Ruins at Palenquea

In Campeche, we visited the fort built in 1719 to defend against pirate attacks before driving to the magnificent Mayan ruins at Uxmal, which was home to some 25,000 inhabitants around 600 AD. The name Uxmal means "thrice-Built" in Mayan, referring to the construction of its highest structure, the Pyramid of the Magician, which stands 117 feet tall.

The Mayans would often build a new temple over an existing one and in this case, five such stages of construction have been found. Indications are that its rulers also presided over the nearby settlements in Kabah, Labna, and Sayil, and there are several roads connecting the sites. The area is known as the Ruta Puuc route, from nearby hills. Carvings most commonly found there include serpents, lattice work and masks of Chac, the god of rain.

Mayas performed human sacrifices at the highest temple of the House of the Magician. With the victim still alive, the priest would rip out the heart with a flint knife and throw the body, allegedly still moving, down the steep steps, rather like the famous scene in Indiana Jones and the Temple of Doom.

Legend held that when a certain gong was sounded, the town of Uxmal would fall to a boy "not born of woman." One day, a dwarf boy who had been raised from an egg by a witch, sounded the gong and stuck fear into the ruler, who ordered him to be executed. The ruler promised the boy's life would be saved if he could perform three impossible tasks, one of which was to build a giant pyramid in a single night. According to the legend, the boy achieved all the tasks and became the new ruler.

The collection of four buildings around a quadrangle was named "Casa de las Monjas," (The Nunnery) by the Spanish, because of the 74 small rooms around the courtyard reminded them of nuns' quarters in a Spanish convent. Each of the four buildings has a unique ornate façade, and each is built on a different level. Regarded by many experts as the best example of Puuc architecture in existence, the Palace of the Governor stands on an artificial raised platform and is thought to be one of the last constructed buildings on the site, built around 987 AD.

Next to the Palace of the Governor and on the same raised platform stands the House of the Turtles, so called because of a frieze of turtles carved around the cornice. It was believed that the turtles suffered along with man during times of great drought, and would also pray to Chac for rain.

Pyramid of the Magician at Uxmal

We spent the night at Chichen Itza, where we visited the famous pyramid of Kukulkan along with the Ball Courts and the temple of Jaguars. Kukulkan means "feathered serpent," and was both the name of a Mayan snake god and an actual Mayan priest who lived in the 10th century.

Chichen Itza has been widely studied, excavated, and restored, moreso than any other Mayan city. The Mayan community thrived there between 700 AD and 900 AD and built most of the structures in the southern area. However, the main buildings in the central area, including the Pyramid of Kukulkan, the Temple of the Warriors and the Ball Court, are Toltec in design and influence. According to Toltec history, in 987 AD the legendary ruler Quetzcoatl (which also means "feathered serpent" in the Nahuatl language – these ancient civilizations really liked their winged snakes) was defeated and expelled from Tula. He was last seen leaving the Gulf coast on a raft of serpents. However, in the same year, Mayan stories recorded the arrival of a king named Kukulkan, the serpent god, whose return had been expected. Kukulkan defeated the Mayan city tribes, and made Chichen Itza his capital.

Towering above other buildings at 79 feet (24 meters) high, the pyramid of Kukulkan has a structured feel about it.

Each side has 91 steps, and adding the platform at the top as a final step, there are 365 in total, one for every day of the year. Further evidence that this building was linked to the Mayan interest in astronomy and the calendar is demonstrated at the spring and autumn equinox. On these days the shadow of the sun playing on the stairs causes the illusion of a snake processing down the pyramid in the direction of the cenote, or sinkhole.

The temple at the top of the pyramid has carvings of Chac the rain god and Quetzalcoatl, the serpent god. Inside there is a sculpture of a jaguar, painted red and with jade eyes.

The Great Ball Court is the largest of its kind in the Mayan world. The length of the playing field there is 400 feet (135 m) and two 25 ft. (8m) high walls run alongside it.

Further east, there is the Temple of the Jaguars with its friezes of the Toltec jaguar emblem, and the Tzompantli, or Platform of the Skulls. It is believed that the Tzompantli was the platform used for the sacrifices resulting from the ball game. Basically, it was like a wine rack, only with human skulls.

Alas, poor Yorick!

The Group of the Thousand Columns complex incorporates the Temple of Warriors and a series of columns, some of which feature carvings of Toltec Warriors, each with the appearance of a different racial type.

Chichen Itza

On the way to Tulum on November 26, we visited the Xkeken Cenote, a popular feature of the Yucatan. Cenotes, as I said, are large sinkholes in the limestone bedrock, usually partly filled with clear water from underground springs. The Mayans believed cenotes led to the underworld. Some are open to the sky, while others are underground caverns. Some scientists believe that they were formed as a result of a giant meteor that hit the Mexican coast at Chicxulub, north of Merida, some 65 million years ago and left the resulting impact crater, which is 120 km. across. It was this ancient event that is thought to have been instrumental in the extinction of dinosaurs.

We stopped at Tulum and visited its ruins dating back to 564 AD. Tulum was a busy Mayan community rather than just a sprawling collection of ceremonial temples, pyramids and palaces. It stood on a bluff overlooking the Caribbean Ocean. The square at center of the city was probably once used for rituals or ceremonies, and is flanked by the Castillo (castle) to the west.

The Castillo, sometimes referred to as the lighthouse, is the tallest building at Tulum and the most famous. The Castillo commands an amazing view of the ocean and coast for miles in both directions. The lintels of its upper rooms are carved with plumed serpent motif. The rooms themselves are of the classic Mayan style.

There are the temples of The Descending God, The Initial Series, and of The Frescos, which is filled with murals. Tulum is completely encircled by a low stone wall, and watchtowers rise from two corners of its western flank, each within reach of an altar.

We continued south, and on the way to Belize we stopped and visited the Mayan ruins at Lamanai, one of the largest sites of its kind, dating back to 1500 BC. The thick, almost writhing vegetation on the path up to the ruins seemed to encase us. There were black howler monkeys in the trees, and we were forewarned about the occasional constrictor, which we saw on the way. It's no wonder snakes and snake gods are such a large part of Mayan mythology.

At Lamanai, over one hundred buildings, including the royal court, have been uncovered over 950 acres. The pyramid there is 33 meters in height and was built around 100 BC.

The Mayans populated Central America for about 2500 years, from 1500 BC until their decline began in the 10th century AD. Some city centers were occupied for another six hundred years when the Spanish arrived. The Mayan empire was bordered on the south by the ruins found in Honduras, on the west by those in Guatemala, and their empire stretched into the Yucatan of Mexico. The Mayan ruins at Lamanai are located in two square areas at the edge of a lush forest reserve. Lamanai is believed to have been occupied from approximately 1500 BC through 1650 AD, and was still inhabited when the Spanish arrived in the 16th century. It is believed that the main temple there was built around 100 BC. Lamanai translates as "submerged crocodile," and many artifacts depicting crocodiles have been found at the site.

The most impressive temples were The Jaguar Temple, named for its boxy jaguar decoration, The Mask Temple, adorned by a 13 ft. stone mask of an ancient Mayan king, and The High Temple, which offers a panoramic view at its summit.

Ruins at Lamanai

Nearly fifty miles off the coast of Belize at the Lighthouse Reef Atoll is the famous Great Blue Hole, an incredible underwater sinkhole. Almost a perfect circle, it measures 100 ft. in diameter and more than 400 ft. deep, and is surrounded by a shallow reef. It was made famous years ago by famed underwater explorer Jacques Cousteau, who called it one of the ten best scuba diving spots in the world.

After passing the Xunantunich Ruins, we entered Guatemala and drove to the Mayan ruins at Tikal in the rainforest of Penn Peninsula. It's one of the most impressive examples of Mayan architecture in Central America. Tikal dates back to 800 BC, and was constantly occupied till about 900 AD. Archeologists have estimated the population between 10,000 and 100,000. The rain forest makes it difficult to determine the real physical extent of the city.

After taking a small ferry across Rio de la Pasion and then driving all day, we arrived in Antigua and checked into the Hotel Atitlan, right on the shore of Lake Atitlan. The next morning we explored the open-air market and saw hundreds of locals in their colorful Mayan clothing gathering around the large town square and its many impressive Colonial buildings.

Shortly after entering Honduras on Dec. 2nd, we visited the Copan ruins, another of Central America's major Mayan sites, marking the southern limit of Maya domination. Copan flourished during the 7th century, and its huge complex consists of several plazas and many temples built on various levels.

First is the Acropolis, which is divided into two large plazas: the West Court and the East Court. The West Court houses two temples and an altar which depicts the 16 members of the Copan Dynasty at its base.

In Nicaragua, we drove to Volcan Masaya, an active volcano steaming with sulfur vapors. When parking near the edge, we were told to back into a somewhat protected space in case of a sudden volcanic eruption.

Nothing like an active volcano to get your attention.

As we entered Costa Rico on December 5th, we saw a lush green landscape that resembled Switzerland. It was clearly a prosperous and beautiful country, and within a few hours we were driving through fruit plantations and botanical gardens and soon passed Arenal Volcano, located in the center of a national park next to Lake de Arenal.

We spent the night in San Jose, Costa Rica's capital city, and the next day we crossed the border into Panama. At the hotel we were greeted by local Panamanian dancers and in the evening, the finishing ceremonies took place over a splendid dinner at Miraflores Restaurant overlooking the locks of the Panama Canal.

Our final Adventure Drive with HERO took place in 2009. I again shipped the 2007 Chevy Tahoe, this time to Singapore, and on February 7th started a 6000 mile drive through South East Asian countries. There were a total of 23 automobiles from all over the world participating. I was accompanied by my brother Reza and my son Darvish.

We left the starting gate early in the morning on February 7th, and at Malacca we checked into the Majestic Hotel. That evening we were all taken by Tuk-Tuks, or motorized rickshaws, to the always busy Jonker Street. where we dined in a Chinese restaurant.

Tuk-Tuks at Majestic Hotel in Malacca

On February 8th, we drove to Kuala Lumpur, the capital of Malaysia and home to the famous Petronas Twin Towers, which were the tallest buildings in the world until 2004, when Taipei 101 was built, which was itself soon surpassed by a structure in Dubai. For dinner we went to the top of the Menara Kuala Lumpur Tower and ate in the revolving restaurant and enjoyed the incredible panoramic views of the city.

As far as the height is concerned, once you get past 100 stories or so, it's all the same to me.

On our way out of the capital, we detoured to Batu Caves, which was an Indian Shrine and a place where over a million Indians had gathered that day to celebrate their New Year. There was a large Buddha in the center of the space, and beyond it 280 steps lead to the sacred cave packed with worshippers.

Batu Caves

Just outside the shrine were thousands of pairs of shoes, all mixed up and piled into a huge mound. There was trash everywhere as the barefoot Indians comingled and prayed together.

I briefly wondered how anyone would ever find their shoes after the ceremony. I guess you'd be lucky to find the right size.

The woodland gradually gave way to tea plantations, and we stopped at Cameron Bharat Teahouse on the way to Cameron Heights and tried some of the local tea. The Cameron Heights were not even discovered until the 1920's, when this beautiful area of green mountains quickly became colonial Malay's leading hill station and tea growing area.

On February 10th, we stopped at the colorful Perak Tong Cave Temples before proceeding to visit the Orangutan Island, where a number of the apes are kept as part of a conservation project. The apes there are being cultivated for release upon maturity into the wild.

A couple of hours after leaving the Orangutan Island and driving on the expressway towards Georgetown, we had a problem with our transmission. The Tahoe basically died on us. We had it towed on a flatbed to a Chevy dealer in Georgetown, only to be told that they did not carry the necessary parts for that kind of vehicle and were unable to repair it.

The next day, February 11th, while the rest of the participants continued the adventure, the three of us were left at the hotel pondering our immediate future and contemplating our options.

With the help of HERO officials and the cooperation of the some of the participants, a plan was worked out for us to fly to Bangkok and rejoin the group, where we would hitch a ride with them.

On February 13th, we flew to Bangkok and awaited the arrival of the others, who started trickling in on February 15th.

The evening before, the three of us took a taxi to the Red-District of Bangkok, well known for its sex shows, among other pursuits. We had heard these shows offered some amusing performances by pretty young girls.

The first place we entered charged us a $20 cover fee and ended up being quite disappointing. A girl stood on a small stage, semi-dressed, darting and bouncing ping-pong balls from between her legs and into a cup, where most, for which I will give her credit, landed on target. But the whole performance was fairly mechanical and without much sex appeal. She looked rather bored to be honest, and there's nothing less sexy than that.

I suppose if I did the same thing a thousand times a night, I might get a little bored, myself.

(NO PICTURE – HAHA)

On February 16th, we all took a guided tour of Bangkok, traveling through the canals and visiting the sites, including the Wat Arun Temple and the Grand Palace.

The Grand Palace in Bangkok

The next day we split up, each of us riding in separate cars with whoever volunteered to take us along. It was all part of the adventure.

On February 18th on the way to Phnom Penh, Cambodia, we stopped at Choeung Ek Genocide Museum, one of Pol

Pot's main killing fields, which is today a place of poignant remembrance. The memorial itself is a tower with glass walls, which house over 8000 skulls of unknown victims. It was a somber experience to see something like that and imagine the lost souls who died there at the hands of that brutal regime.

In Phnom Penh we also visited the Tuol Sleng Genocide Museum or S-21, which had been a high school that was converted during the regime of Pol Pot to a center for detention, interrogation, torture and execution. It basically became a secret prison.

Security Prison 21, as it was also known, began as a place of learning, became a place of horror, and now teaches us the error of man's inhumanity to man. I would say it came full circle, as most such places eventually do.

S-21 building

Also of interest was our visit to the Royal Palace, which was constructed in 1866 and is comprised of a number of buildings, including The Silver Pagoda which houses a golden Buddha adorned with thousands of diamonds.

That place is truly a girl's best friend.

The day after we arrived in Siem Reap in northwestern Cambodia, we visited the Floating Village, which consists of hundreds of homes floating on Tonle Sap Lake, the largest freshwater lake in Southeast Asia.

Floating Village

In the afternoon we went to the majestic Angkor Temples. This series of gigantic structures, including Angkor Wat, were built during the 12th century by Suryavarman II, symbolizing the mythic Mt. Mera, and is a symbolic representation of Hindu cosmology. In the evening, HERO arranged a dinner in a temple setting resembling a movie soundstage, with colorful performers dancing to the local music for our entertainment.

Once more, HERO showed us they really knew how to part.

Returning to Thailand on February 24th, we visited the ancient city of Sukhathai (1200 AD), which showcases a giant Buddha surrounded by a moat. Recognized as the first kingdom, the city of Sukhathai gained prominence and its independence in 1238. Nine kings ruled over an expanding area, and the city was annexed in 1376 by the ruler of Ayutthaya.

Angkor Wat Temple

The most famous king of Sukhathai was Ramkamhaeng the Great, under whose rule the Thai alphabet was developed and under whom the city influence extended beyond its borders.

Giant Buddha at Sukhathai

In the afternoon, we stopped at the 900 year old Buddhist Temple of Wat Phra That Lampang Luang in Lampang. To enter the temple, you must first pass a pair of guardian lions and climb the Naga stairway up to the massive gate. The main prayer hall, Wiharn Luang, stands close inside the main entrance and you are required to take your shoes off before entering. Lucky for us there were not as many people there as back in Kuala Lumpur.

Sturdy columns, finished in black lacquer and stenciled with gold leaf designs, support the roof.

At the back of the Wihan Luang sits a massive gilded Ku, a sort of prang sheltering the main Buddha image, which was Phra Chao Land Thong and cast in 1563. On either side of the Ku are throne-like pulpits, sometimes used by monks but more often used to house other Buddha images on important ceremonial occasions.

Behind the main prayer hall stands the 45 meter tall Chedi, whose face is covered with copper and bronze sheets, which over the centuries have oxidized into a variety of green and blue shades. It's actually quite beautiful.

Later that day, we visited the Thai Elephant Conservation Center, where a group of pachyderms put on quite a show for us. They rolled and picked heavy logs, painted beautiful flowers on paper using their trunk to hold the brush. The paint was applied to the brush by their trainer. The elephants actually seemed to be having fun.

They were much more into their work than the girl with the ping-pong balls, that's for sure.

Afterwards we drove to Chaing Mae for our overnight stop.

The next day we were taken to Mae Taeng, where we took rides on ox-carts and elephants, and then floated on bamboo rafts down the river for a few hours. It was another of those once-in-a-lifetime experiences during a trip filled with them.

On the way back we stopped at Kayan Village to see "the Long Necks." Like many tribes in Africa, they endeavor to stretch their necks, one ring at a time. The rings are snapped around the necks of girls beginning at the age of six. A few rings may be added every year up to a limit of 20.

Elephant Painting

The women's necks aren't actually stretched, but the weight of the rings gradually crushes their collar bones, producing the illusion of long necks. The neck seems eerily elongated and makes the woman look like a giraffe. The rings are only removed on their wedding night.

If I was a girl there I suppose I would be pretty eager to find a husband. It reminded me of the old joke about a fellow who asks his friend, a marathon runner, why he keeps running.

"Because it feels so good when I stop."

Long Necks

On February 28th, we arrived at Vientiane in Laos, with its L'arc de Triumph victory gate clearly displaying the influence of the French.

After spending the next night at Luang Probang in Laos and visiting its temples, we drove to Dien Ben Phu, Vietnam. We toured the sites and visited the remains of the battle where the Vietnamese defeated the French in 1954 to gain their independence, thus changing the course of history in Southeast Asia.

After passing many rice fields and seeing the women with their traditional cone shaped hats, we arrived in the dirty city of Hanoi on March 5th.

The next day we drove to Ha Long Bay and took an overnight junket on the South China Sea. Dinner that night was served in a beautifully decorated and cave, where local dancers put on quite a show for us.

Junket on the South China Sea

We entered China on March 7th, and the next day attended the finishing ceremony in Zhuhai, China. We spent two nights in Macau, the gambling Mecca of Asia, with 27 truly unbelievable casinos, before flying home from Hong Kong.

My next "Adventure Drive" in planned for the spring of 2011 through the Baltics and Scandinavian countries. Since HERO principals retired, we had to put this trip together ourselves with the help of an English couple who had participated in the past drives. Only four automobiles will be sharing in this drive, all experienced drivers from prior drives.

My brother Reza will accompany me and we plan to take a train ride from Helsinki to St. Petersburg in Russia to observe the wonderful creations of Peter the Great and the subsequent accumulation of artwork by Catherine the Great in the Hermitage museum.

By the time I reached 70 years of age, I came to the personal conclusion that, in contrast to my own calm and collective demeanor, women are from another planet and for most part they can be quite irrational and demanding, which makes them quite difficult to live with. Especially at that age.

So, having gone through one marriage and a few relationships, some long, some short, I've decided to spend my remaining days on my own. I've had a good life, worked hard, made some money, and now I just want to socialize, travel, and play poker.

But no man can live completely alone, and so I decided for my 70th birthday to take another companion. On that day, I began what I hope will be a long-term, satisfying relationship with:

My 2010 Ferrari California

Writing a book of this type naturally leads to reflection on one's life, and I am certainly no exception. Like all those who reach my age, I have lived through triumph and tragedy, loved and lost, and both endured and enjoyed the full range of the human experience.

Mostly as I look back, I stand amazed at how the world has changed since I was boy in Isfahan. As I write this book in the spring of 2011, the land of my birth is going through tumultuous times; indeed, the entire region is, as well as the world.

But as I reflect on how the world is changing, I am struck by how things remain the same. It is always about the yearning of individuals to find a better life. No matter the advances in finance or science, or technology, it all boils down to the basic human desire to follow one's dreams, and that's what I've always done, no matter my circumstances.

A lot has changed since my most fervent dream was my own bicycle to ride through the rutted lanes of Isfahan, but you could say that my hopes today are much the same. Perhaps a bicycle to a poor Iranian boy in the 1950's is not all that different from a Ferrari to a successful businessman today. It's not the cost, but the desire.

Always follow your dreams, because you never know where they will lead.

CPSIA information can be obtained at www.ICGtesting.com
Printed in the USA
242910LV00004B/1/P